MACROECONOMICS

THE BASICS

Macroeconomics: The Basics provides a concise, accessible treatment of the subject, using an economics framework to analyze the theories, policies, and applications of the field.

Organized in six parts, the book covers the most important areas in macroeconomics, including national income, unemployment and inflation, economic growth, savings, investment, the financial system, money and banking, money and inflation, aggregate expenditures, aggregate demand and supply, fiscal policy, monetary policy, international trade, and international finance. Written in a highly engaging style by an established economist, each chapter is accompanied by key terminology lists to emphasize the important terms and concepts, as well as further reading suggestions to enable deeper exploration of the specific topics.

Providing the reader with a solid foundation of the basic principles of macroeconomics and establishing a framework for further study, *Macroeconomics: The Basics* is essential reading for any student or professional interested in learning about the field.

Thomas R. Sadler is Professor of Economics at Western Illinois University. He teaches courses on the Fundamentals of Economic Theory, Environmental Economics, Energy Economics, Principles of Economics, and the Chicago Economy. His research focuses on environmental policy, energy economics, professional sports leagues, and high-performance organizations.

The Basics

The Basics is a highly successful series of accessible guidebooks which provide an overview of the fundamental principles of a subject area in a jargon-free and undaunting format.

Intended for students approaching a subject for the first time, the books both introduce the essentials of a subject and provide an ideal springboard for further study. With over 50 titles spanning subjects from artificial intelligence (AI) to women's studies, *The Basics* are an ideal starting point for students seeking to understand a subject area.

Each text comes with recommendations for further study and gradually introduces the complexities and nuances within a subject.

BIOANTHROPOLOGY
MARC KISSEL

NEW YORK CITY
KATRIN B. ANACKER

HISTORICAL GEOGRAPHIES
PAUL GRIFFIN AND CHERYL MCGEACHAN

ANCIENT WARFARE
CONOR WHATELY

MARKETING
KARL MOORE, NIKETH PAREEK, MARIE PARENT AND MISAKO FURUYA

UNLOCKING BUSINESS INSIGHTS
ANEESH BANERJEE

MACROECONOMICS
THOMAS R. SADLER

For more information about this series, please visit: www.routledge.com/The-Basics/book-series/B

MACROECONOMICS

THE BASICS

Thomas R. Sadler

Routledge
Taylor & Francis Group

LONDON AND NEW YORK

Designed cover image: StudioM1 / Getty Images ®

First published 2026
by Routledge
4 Park Square, Milton Park, Abingdon, Oxon OX14 4RN

and by Routledge
605 Third Avenue, New York, NY 10158

Routledge is an imprint of the Taylor & Francis Group, an informa business

British Library Cataloguing-in-Publication Data
A catalogue record for this book is available from the British Library

ISBN: 978-1-041-15289-7 (hbk)
ISBN: 978-1-041-15287-3 (pbk)
ISBN: 978-1-003-67870-0 (ebk)

DOI: 10.4324/9781003678700

Typeset in Bembo
by Taylor & Francis Books

Access the Support Material: www.routledge.com/9781041152873

To Holly, Maya, and Mathew with love.

CONTENTS

FIGURES

TABLES

ACKNOWLEDGEMENTS

I thank Routledge for publishing this book. At every step of the writing process, Chloe Herbert and Michelle Gallagher provided helpful feedback and encouragement. It is a pleasure working with such responsive partners in publishing.

Professionally, I benefit from the interaction with many individuals. My mentors include William Kleiner, David Loshky, and Robert Bohm. My colleagues include Anne Bynoe, Bette Lott, John Tomer, Tara Feld, Jessica Lin, Alla Melkumian, Shane Sanders, Bhavneet Walia, William Koch, Manda Tiwari, and Braxton Gately. Thank you for the conversations about economics and life.

Personally, I enjoy the support from a wonderful family, including Judy, Charles, Laura, Chris, Mark, Fred, and Rick.

I dedicate this book and all of my work to Holly, Maya, and Mathew. I love you very much.

Thomas R. Sadler

AN OVERVIEW OF THE BOOK

The book includes six parts. Chapter 1 introduces the topic of macroeconomics. Part I considers the measuring of macroeconomic outcomes, including national income (Chapter 2), unemployment (Chapter 3), and inflation (Chapter 4). Part II addresses the foundations of economic growth, including economic growth (Chapter 5) and savings, investment, and the financial system (Chapter 6). Part III introduces monetary economics, with material on money and banking (Chapter 7) and money and inflation (Chapter 8). Part IV presents the topic of cyclical instability, including aggregate expenditures (Chapter 9) and aggregate demand and supply (Chapter 10). Part V discusses stabilization policy, including fiscal policy (Chapter 11) and monetary policy (Chapter 12). Part VI on international economics considers international trade (Chapter 13) and international finance (Chapter 14). In Parts V and VI, instructors may cover the chapters in any order.

INTRODUCTION TO MACROECONOMICS

MACROECONOMIC THINKING

Macroeconomics is the study of the economy as a whole. When macroeconomists address economic problems and challenges, they consider broad trends throughout the economy, including the growth rate, change in the price level, and movement of the unemployment rate. By studying these trends, they are able to assess whether the macroeconomy is achieving its three main goals: growth in the production of output, a stable price level, and a low unemployment rate. When the economy achieves these goals, firms are producing more goods and services, prices are increasing at a low and predictable rate, and workers who are actively seeking jobs are able to find employment. But the macroeconomy does not always achieve the goals.

During 2020, when the coronavirus pandemic spread throughout the world, many non-essential forms of economic activity shut down, including entertainment facilities, restaurants, and shopping malls. Individuals sheltered in place. Firms moved economic activity online. Governments provided aid. But problems persisted. A rise in morbidity and mortality threatened healthcare systems. Supply chain disruptions reduced the ability to transport goods around the world. A reduction in educational services altered household activity, creating the need to find new forms of childcare and methods to work from home.

During this time, macroeconomic problems emerged. By the end of the first quarter of 2020, the production of output plummeted in the United States (US). Many firms struggled to maintain

DOI: 10.4324/9781003678700-1

their *production process*, the method in which they turned economic resources into output. Economic resources, which are the factors of production, serve as the inputs that produce goods and services, including *land* (natural resources and geographic locations), *labor* (workers in the production process), *capital* (the physical capital such as machines and equipment that contribute to the production of output and human capital, the economic value of an individual's skills) and *entrepreneurship* (the process of identifying new opportunities and bringing together the appropriate economic resources). As a result of the decrease in production, many firms laid off workers. The unemployment rate in the US skyrocketed, rising from 4.4 percent in March 2020 to 14.7 percent in April 2020. The increase of more than 10 percent meant that millions of people lost their jobs.

Over time, however, another problem emerged: a high rate of inflation. In economics, inflation means the rate at which the prices of goods and services increase in a specific time period, such as a year. Two forces contributed to the problem.

On the supply side, the disruptions in global supply chains from the pandemic led to shortages of many goods, including common household items. Countries closed their borders. Food shortages complicated the ability of households to satisfy their basic needs. These forces put upward pressure on prices.

On the demand side, federal governments addressed the problems of declining production and rising unemployment. They implemented aid packages. In the US, the federal government provided aid. During 2020 and 2021, the federal government sent three stimulus checks to households, boosting their spending. In an economy that was starting to recover from the pandemic, the spending put upward pressure on prices.

Between 2021 and 2023, a large increase in the price level resulted from these outcomes. But then many households struggled to pay the higher prices, especially for food, gasoline, and rent. The results were severe, including a loss in household purchasing power, financial strain for low-income households, a decline in consumer confidence, and a higher level of economic instability.

This book, *Macroeconomics: The Basics*, discusses the field of macroeconomics, including economic growth, inflation, unemployment, and many other macroeconomic topics. As a reader, you will learn about macroeconomic tools and concepts, establishing the knowledge necessary to understand the field. For readers who do not have a background in economics, the book is written as an introduction.

In an engaging manner, the book introduces new concepts and applies them to contemporary applications. For example, a discussion of market outcomes creates a framework for the economic way of thinking. A *market* is a mechanism that brings together buyers and sellers for the purpose of exchange. Markets are physical or electric mechanisms. But the book also emphasizes that, in markets, a limited quantity of economic resources exists. The limit establishes a context for the basic economic problem: how to allocate scarce resources among unlimited wants. By discussing these and many other topics, the book provides a solid foundation of the principles of the field and establishes a framework for further study. Moving forward, however, it is important to discuss the use of models in the field of economics.

MODELS IN ECONOMICS

A model is a simplification of reality. Individuals may have a favorite model car, plane, or train. But economists use equations or graphical models to understand economic activity. In economics, models demonstrate the relationship between important variables. Their simplicity allows economists to focus on one change at a time, using the *ceteris paribus* assumption that other conditions remain the same. An example is the relationship between consumption and income. In models that analyze household spending, when income rises, consumption rises. But other variables also impact household consumption, including future expectations and public policy.

PRODUCTION POSSIBILITIES

Another example of an economic model is the *production possibility curve* (PPC). The model demonstrates the maximum amount of output that an economy may produce, given the current level of economic resources and *production technology*. Production technology refers to the tools and techniques that produce goods and services, including economic resources, processes of automation, data analysis, and artificial intelligence (AI). A technological advancement occurs when an improvement in one or more of these areas leads to either a higher level of production or a lower cost.

The PPC demonstrates two economic principles. First, at one point in time, the economy's productive capacity is limited. The reason is that the economy has a certain amount of economic resources. Even though population growth may occur, the economy is constrained in the present by the total number of workers. The same constraint exists for capital. Second, when the economy allocates scarce economic resources to produce goods and services, the resources cannot produce other forms of output. The output that is not produced represents the *opportunity cost*, the value of the best foregone alternative. Using scarce resources to produce more electric vehicles, for example, means fewer resources for vehicles with combustion engines. Allocating more resources for the production of solar and wind power means fewer resources for power derived from fossil fuels. While economic, environmental, and social reasons motivate these decisions, an opportunity cost results from the choice of producing one form of output over another.

DRAWING THE PPC

The PPC demonstrates the scarcity of economic resources. As a result, tradeoffs occur. To illustrate this principle, economists draw a PPC as a simplified economy producing two goods. Suppose the economy produces consumption goods and capital goods (Figure 1.1). The unit

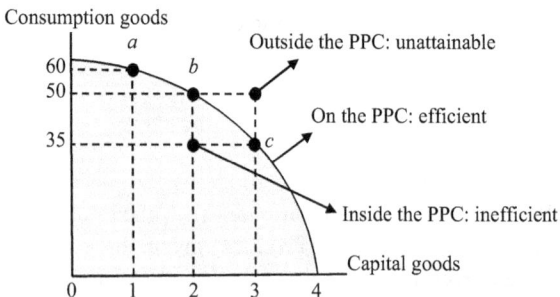

Figure 1.1 Production possibility curve

of measurement is in the millions. Consumption goods, such as durables, non-durables, and services, are consumed in the present. Capital goods, such as computers, machinery, and equipment, are the physical economic resources used by firms to produce output over time. Even though the PPC has a concave shape (bowed out away from the origin), signaling an increasing opportunity cost, the PPC may also be a straight line, corresponding to a constant opportunity cost.

The production frontier, which includes points *a*, *b*, and *c*, demonstrates the maximum annual quantity of consumption goods the economy produces, given the quantity of capital goods. The model establishes production possibilities: if the economy produces 1 million capital goods, it also produces 60 million consumption goods (point *a*). If it produces 2 million capital goods, it also produces 50 million consumption goods (point *b*), and so on. But an important distinction exists between points on the PPC, outside the PPC, and inside the PPC.

EFFICIENCY AND POTENTIAL OUTPUT

With points on the PPC, the economy allocates economic resources efficiently and produces its potential output. An *efficient* point of production exists with no missed opportunities. There is no way to produce more of one good without producing less of the other good. The economy reaches its potential. As long as the economy produces on the PPC, it is achieving an efficient outcome. At point *c*, 35 million consumption goods are the maximum feasible quantity if the economy commits to producing 3 million capital goods.

A point outside the PPC, such as 3 million capital goods and 50 million consumption goods, is not feasible in the present. The economy does not have enough economic resources or the technological capability to produce beyond the frontier. Given the current level of economic resources and technology, points outside of the PPC are unattainable. To reach a point outside of the PPC, the economy must experience economic growth or the gains from trade.

A point inside the PPC, such as 2 million capital goods and 35 million consumption goods, is feasible but inefficient. The economy is not using its economic resources and/or technological capabilities to their fullest extent. That is, the economy could produce more of one good without sacrificing the production of the other good. Points inside the PPC represent an under-employment of economic resources. The economy is not producing at its potential.

OPPORTUNITY COST

The PPC is a useful model to demonstrate that the real cost of a choice is what is given up in order to achieve it. If the economy moves from point *a* to point *b*, it will produce 1 million more capital goods, but 10 million fewer consumption goods. As a result, the opportunity cost of 1 capital good is 10 consumption goods, the output that is foregone by making the move.

Is the opportunity cost of more capital goods the same along this PPC? The answer is no. If the economy moves from point *b* to point *c*, the capital goods increase from 2 million to 3 million; however, the consumption goods decrease from 50 million to 35 million. In this range, the opportunity cost of producing 1 million more capital goods is 15 million consumption goods. Compared to moving from point *a* to point *b*, the opportunity cost rises.

In this situation, the economy experiences an *increasing opportunity cost*. The more capital goods the economy produces, the more costly it becomes in terms of foregone consumption goods. The same principle holds true for a movement in the other direction. Producing more consumption goods along the PPC leads to an increasing opportunity cost in terms of foregone capital goods. When the opportunity cost is increasing, the PPC assumes the concave shape.

What is the economic reason for increasing opportunity cost? Along the PPC, when the economy allocates more resources for the production of a specific form of output, it is diverting resources from the production of other forms of output. As production shifts, the economic resources that are diverted become less suited to their new tasks. The opportunity cost continues to rise for each new good or service produced. The idea is that certain economic resources are suited to produce specific forms of output. When production moves economic resources from their areas of focus, productivity declines.

Economists also draw the PPC as a straight line. In this case, a movement along the PPC leads to a *constant opportunity cost*. The cost of producing more output remains constant, regardless of the initial production bundle. With a straight line, the economy produces different production bundles without altering the opportunity cost. The assumption is that economic resources are equally suited to all production processes.

The PPC describes resource allocation, tradeoffs, and production possibilities. But it does not include all aspects of the macroeconomy. (Each chapter in the book expands the model of the macroeconomy.) By demonstrating several important points, however, the PPC is useful. First, the PPC shows that, in the present, the economy may produce its potential output on the frontier, given the economic resources and technology. Second, with an inefficient allocation of economic resources, the economy does not produce the potential output. Third, over time, the economy may produce a bundle that is currently outside of the PPC. The next section discusses this possibility.

SHIFTS IN THE PPC

Economists use the PPC to demonstrate *economic growth*, the ability of the economy to produce more output. Because the production of output is a function of economic resources and technology, an increase in these factors leads to economic growth. For example, the population of the US increases every year. As a result, the number of potential workers grows. All else equal, more workers means that the economy may produce more goods and services.

In general, when the quantity of economic resources increases, and the resources are used productively, economic growth occurs. Technological progress—an improvement in the technical means of producing output—also leads to economic growth. When firms innovate or implement AI to enhance decision making, they produce more output, given their economic resources.

In the model, additional economic resources or technological advancements shift the PPC outward. When this process occurs, the economy produces more consumption goods and capital goods. The PPC may also shift when an economy realizes the gains from trade. While the latter process is discussed in the following section, these possibilities are summarized here:

- When the quantity of economic resources increases, the PPC shifts out
- In the presence of technological advancements in production, the PPC shifts out
- When an economy realizes the gains from trade, the PPC shifts out

A focus on the production of capital goods enhances the process of economic growth When an economy produces more capital goods, it prioritizes future productivity over present consumption. In Figure 1.2, suppose the economy produces at point b, rather than point a, on $PPC_{present}$. The choice puts the economy in a position to expand its potential output over time. The reason is that when firms have more capital goods, productivity rises.

At point b, the allocation of resources for machines, equipment, and computer systems increases the economy's future production capacity, shifting the PPC away from the origin. In the present, the opportunity cost is fewer consumption goods. But over time the rate of economic growth is higher, reflecting the fact that the $PPC_{future.B}$ is further from the origin than $PPC_{future.A}$.

In addition to more economic resources and technological advancements, another factor leads to an outward shift of the PPC: the gains from trade, the subject of the next section.

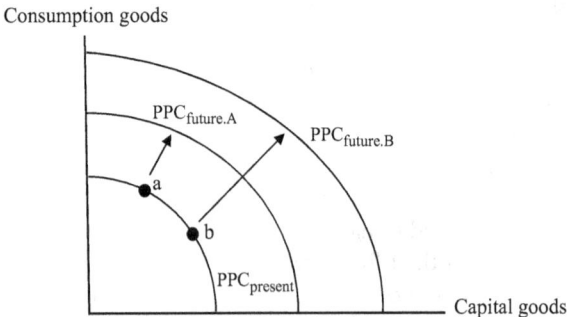

Figure 1.2 Economic growth

THE GAINS FROM TRADE

Countries establish *open economies* that conduct trade with the rest of the world. Some countries export a wide variety of goods and services, while other countries focus on a smaller number of items. A larger economy may export industrial forms of output and services. But a smaller economy may export agricultural products, natural resources, and tourism.

The gains from trade stem from the division of labor, which leads to *specialization*. When individuals specialize, the economy enhances its productive capacity. Specialization is the reason that individuals build their skill sets and focus on specific careers in areas such as business, education, or the law.

Markets create the context for specialization. Because markets exist for all goods, producers are able to sell the items they produce. The same market reality holds true for services, such as banking, entertainment, and management. In the presence of markets, economic agents specialize, forgo self-sufficiency, and purchase what they need. When countries specialize in specific goods and services that they are good at producing and exchange them for other forms of output, they experience the gains from trade.

Specialization and trade focus on the principle of *comparative advantage*: the ability to produce output at a lower domestic opportunity cost than a trading partner. A comparative advantage means that a country sacrifices fewer economic resources during production than a trading partner. The principle stems from cost, quality, and characteristics such as geography and climate.

Comparative advantage differs from *absolute advantage*: the ability to produce a larger quantity of output. The US has absolute advantage in the production of many forms of output; however, a smaller country may have a comparative advantage in certain products. Because of its Caribbean climate, the Dominican Republic has a comparative advantage in the production of bananas. Because of its tropical climate, Brazil has a comparative advantage in the production of sugarcane. Because of its semiconductor manufacturing, Taiwan has a comparative advantage in microchips. Many other examples exist.

Comparative advantage, not absolute advantage, serves as the basis for trade. When a country gives up fewer economic resources to produce output, and trades with other countries, it experiences economic gains. In the model, when the gains from trade occur, the PPC shifts out.

The result is that countries export the products with a comparative advantage and import the products they need. Today, *closed economies*, when countries do not participate in international trade or financial exchange, are rare.

USING ECONOMIC MODELS

This chapter demonstrates that economists use the principles of scarcity and opportunity cost to create models of economic activity. In macroeconomics, the models explain the functioning of the economy as a whole. The models also demonstrate the relationship between important variables, such as economic resources, technology, and output. But economists also use economic models to forecast the outcome of economic policy.

POSITIVE AND NORMATIVE ECONOMICS

During the coronavirus pandemic of 2020–2022, the US government sent stimulus checks to households, as the chapter's introduction explains. The households were instructed to use the money to purchase goods and services, thus stimulating economic activity. At the time, several policy questions existed:

- How much would the checks cost?
- How much economic activity would the policy generate?
- Should the federal government implement a different policy?

The first two questions differ from the third question. The first two questions are objective, involving facts. After a policy is implemented, it is possible to calculate its cost. In addition, the change in economic activity depends on the size of the multiplier effect, a concept addressed later in the book. The point is that economists make specific calculations to answer the first two questions.

But the third question is subjective. Policy analysts have competing views. Certain analysts may answer yes to the third question, but others may disagree.

The questions highlight two approaches. First, the analysis that addresses facts refers to *positive economics* or "what is." As long as the answers to the first two questions remain factual, they serve as examples of positive economics. Second, *normative economics* considers economic prescription or "what ought to be." This approach, which entails opinion, refers to the subjective and value-based study of economics. Both approaches have a place. But it's important to establish the difference between the two. It's also important to support opinions with facts.

MECHANISMS OF CHOICE

Economies are defined by the answers to three questions: What does the economy produce? How does the economy produce? For whom does the economy produce? The economic system provides the answers. Today, *capitalism* serves as the world's most important economic system. Capitalism exerts power and influence over the process of resource allocation. In a capitalist system, markets establish economic incentives, determining an economy's methods of exchange and industrial organization. In the system, market incentives influence the firms that decide what to produce and how to produce. The distribution of output determines for whom the output flows.

In this system, no central planner exists. As Adam Smith, the foremost classical economist, wrote in *The Wealth of Nations* (1776), the *invisible hand of the market* guides economic activity. The concept describes how markets operate. If prices rise, firms have the incentive to bring more output to the market. If sales rise, their profits increase. In capitalism, decentralized economic decisions occur, according to changing economic conditions.

But an economy may establish an unequal distribution of income among individuals in the country. Some people have a lot more income than others. In capitalism, the owners of the means of production—the economic resources and processes used to produce goods and services—benefit the most from the existing order. The capitalists have a greater potential to accumulate assets. While economic growth may benefit everyone by increasing the size of the economic pie, in reality the government must redistribute income to establish a more equal distribution of income.

The invisible hand moves the economy along the PPC. If consumers demand more consumption goods, the economy moves from point *c* in Figure 1.1 to point *b*, or from point *b* to point *a*. While the movement along the PPC entails an opportunity cost of foregone capital goods, consumer preference prevails.

Today, we identify the invisible hand as the *market mechanism*. It does not require a central planner. With the market mechanism, the price signal provides the incentive for both production and consumption. If individuals have a sufficient amount of income, they will purchase the goods and services in which they have both a willingness and ability to pay. If prices rise, producers take advantage of the potential for profit. They allocate economic resources for the production of specific forms of output, such as electronic devices or entertainment services. In the process, the invisible hand of the market prevails.

In his famous book, Adam Smith was so inspired by the invisible hand that he advocated for a *laissez-faire* policy in which the government should leave the market alone. By allocating economic resources in an optimal way, according to Smith, the capitalist system served as the most efficient form of economic organization.

As *Macroeconomics: The Basics* explains, however, sometimes the market does not lead to an optimal outcome. An example is the coronavirus pandemic and corresponding economic downturn. When unemployment rises and production falls, the government should intervene.

KEY TERMS

absolute advantage
capital
capitalism
ceteris paribus
closed economies
comparative advantage
constant opportunity cost
economic growth
efficient
entrepreneurship
increasing opportunity cost

invisible hand of the market
labor
laissez-faire
land
macroeconomics
market
market mechanism
normative economics
open economies
opportunity cost
positive economics
production possibility curve
production process
production technology
specialization

FURTHER READING

Almudi, Isabel and Fatas-Villafranca, Francisco. 2018. "Promotion and Coevolutionary Dynamics in Contemporary Capitalism." *Journal of Economic Issues*, 52 (1): 80–102.

Binder, Carola and Kamdar, Rupal. 2022. "Expected and Realized Inflation in Historical Perspective." *Journal of Economic Perspectives*, 36 (3): 131–156.

Malmendier, Ulrike and Taylor, Timothy. 2015. "On the Verges of Overconfidence." *Journal of Economic Perspectives*, 29 (4): 3–8.

PART I

MEASURING MACROECONOMIC OUTCOMES

NATIONAL INCOME

CHANGES IN THE MACROECONOMY

During this century, the United States (US) has experienced periods of economic growth, an increase in the production of output. But in 2001, the collapse of the dot-com bubble in the stock market led to an economic downturn that lasted eight months. During the downturn, production declined. Even though the downturn was mild, younger workers experienced a decrease in employment that lasted for years.

From 2002 to 2007, an economic expansion contributed to an increase in both output and income. But the period led to rising housing prices, lax lending standards by banks, and a subprime mortgage crisis. The latter occurred when lenders provided loans to individuals who could not afford to pay them back.

From 2008 to 2009, the Great Recession served as the largest downturn since the Great Depression of the 1930s. The economic outcomes included a sharp rise in the unemployment rate, housing market collapse, decrease in stock portfolios, and loss of household wealth. By the middle of 2009, the economy began to recover with the passage of the American Recovery and Reinvestment Act, a policy implemented by the federal government to jumpstart the economy. Compared to previous downturns, the recovery was slow. It took the economy nearly four years to reach its previous high in production.

The economic growth that began in 2009 lasted a decade. The expansion led to the creation of millions of new jobs, an increase

DOI: 10.4324/9781003678700-3

in production, and higher incomes for households across the income spectrum. By the end of 2019, the unemployment rate was at a fifty-year low.

But at the beginning of 2020, the coronavirus pandemic ravaged economies around the world. As the previous chapter explains, the crisis threatened the healthcare and economic systems. Workers in low-wage occupations experienced persistent economic burdens. From a macroeconomic perspective, a brief downturn occurred in March and April of 2020. Because of the intervention measures of the federal government, the expansion that followed the pandemic downturn led to job creation and rising levels of household income.

The management of the economy presents an ongoing challenge. The important components, including income, output, and prices, change according to market forces, beyond the control of the government. Because of the interconnection between the economies of different countries, the problems in one economy may spread to other economies. With the ability of both firms and workers to relocate, market competition persists. In some countries, population growth increases the size of the labor force, impacting consumer demand. But population decline in others leads to labor shortages and a decrease in production.

Markets and institutions influence macroeconomic outcomes (Figure 2.1). *Factor markets* establish the supply and demand conditions for economic resources, which are the factors of production. Firms employ the resources to produce output, which is bought and sold in *product markets*. Financial institutions such as commercial banks provide financial services to firms and individuals, including loans and financial investments. The government implements policies that alter spending patterns, the tax code, interest rates, and the money supply.

The study of macroeconomics demonstrates that economies experience periods of growth and decline. Two questions emerge: Why does this pattern occur? How do economists measure the changes in production? By analyzing the cycle of economic activity, macroeconomic performance, and aggregate output, this chapter answers the questions.

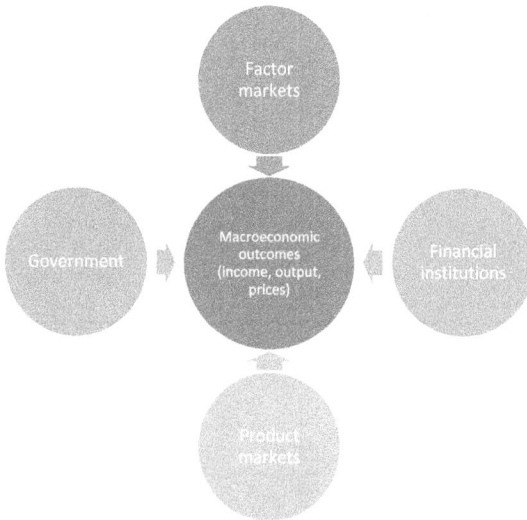

Figure 2.1 Markets and institutions

CYCLE OF ECONOMIC ACTIVITY

The *business cycle* includes periods of economic expansion and contraction. As a feature of economic activity, the business cycle demonstrates short-run fluctuations in the production of output. It includes four phases: expansion, peak, contraction, and trough (Figure 2.2). The expansionary phase entails economic growth, rising employment, and more consumer spending. When the economy operates at capacity, the peak occurs. The contractionary phase entails lower levels of production, rising unemployment, and less consumer spending. In a contraction, firms curtail hiring and lay off workers, contributing to the downturn. The trough is the lowest point.

In the business cycle, the expansionary phase is normally longer than the contractionary phase. But each business cycle is different (Table 2.1). In the US, since 1950, the contractions have lasted between 2 months and 18 months. Some contractions are *recessions*, significant downturns in economic activity that last more than a few months. The expansions have varied between 12 months and

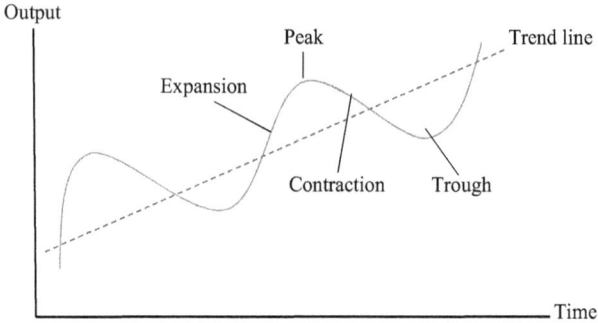

Figure 2.2 Business cycle

Table 2.1 Business cycles in the US since 1950

Years	Peak	Trough	Contraction (months)	Expansion (months)
1953–1954	July 1953	May 1954	10	39
1957–1958	August 1957	April 1958	8	24
1960–1961	April 1960	February 1961	10	106
1969–1970	December 1969	November 1970	11	36
1973–1975	November 1973	March 1975	16	58
1980	January 1980	July 1980	6	12
1981–1982	July 1981	November 1982	16	92
1990–1991	July 1990	March 1991	8	120
2001	March 2001	November 2001	8	73
2007–2009	December 2007	June 2009	18	128
2020	February 2020	April 2020	2	—

128 months. The expansions lead to an increase in economic activity, including income, output, and prices. The trend line slopes upward: each new peak is higher than the previous peak, demonstrating economic growth.

Why do business cycles occur? In the expansionary phase, consumer confidence rises. Household spending increases. Because sales increase, firms experience a decline in inventories. As a result, production rises. Workers are hired. But eventually firms reach their capacity. At the same time, prices rise, slowing down consumer spending. Over time, business inventories rise, production falls, and the unemployment rate increases. The contractionary phase begins.

In order to smooth the business cycle, the government may intervene. The objective is to lengthen the expansion or shorten the contraction. During the coronavirus pandemic, the stimulus packages of the federal government of the US achieved the latter objective.

MACROECONOMIC PERFORMANCE

When macroeconomists evaluate whether the economy is achieving economic growth, low unemployment, and price-level stability, they look to *national income accounts*. In the US, the Bureau of Economic Analysis (BEA) tabulates and publishes the data on output, income, and prices. The information determines the relative strength of the economy, tracks the business cycle, and compares the economy's performance to that of other countries. In 1934, a group of economists working with Simon Kuznets reported to the US Senate on the creation of economic aggregates, summary statistics of the nation's economic activity. The statistics included consumer spending, business investment, and national output. By 1947, the BEA had created the main components of the national income and product accounts (NIPA). In 1971, Kuznets won the Nobel Prize in Economics for this work.

NATIONAL INCOME AND PRODUCT ACCOUNTS

Using the NIPA, economists evaluate the economy's performance. By aggregating the country's economic activity, they determine the NIPA. Using information from the NIPA, the *circular flow of economic activity* demonstrates the equivalence of spending and output (Figure 2.3).

In the circular flow model, firms and households interact in the product and resource markets. The product market includes the supply of and demand for goods and services, prices, and changes in market conditions. Households provide the economic resources (land, labor, capital, entrepreneurship) for the production of output. Firms provide the payments for the economic resources

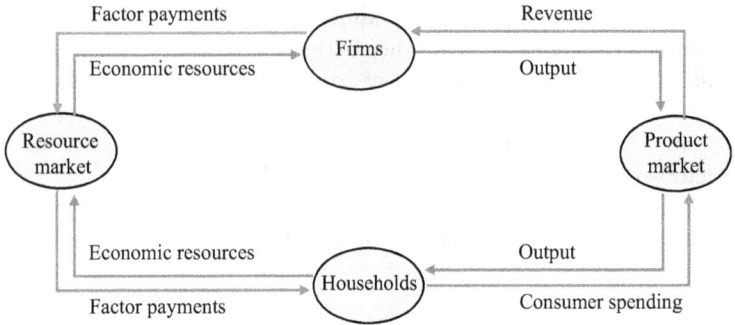

Figure 2.3 Circular flow of economic activity

that are bought and sold in the resource market. An example is the wages that laborers receive for their work effort. Firms produce the output that is purchased by households. In turn, households provide consumer spending, which becomes sales revenue for the firms. In the circular flow diagram, consumer spending is equivalent to the production of output. That is, all of the dollars spent in the economy become income.

SPENDING AND INCOME

The circular flow of economic activity demonstrates the origin of aggregate income and output. In the model, consumers buy goods and services in the product market. In the real economy, however, the government and foreign buyers also purchase goods and services. Firms spend money on investment goods such as machines, equipment, and computer systems. The spending by the government, foreign buyers, and firms exists in the NIPA. But it is not included in the circular flow model. The income generated in the resource market flows to households. Different types of income exist (Table 2.2). Households are the owners of the factors of production.

NATIONAL OUTPUT

An economy's *Gross Domestic Product* (GDP) is the total market value of goods and services produced in the economy in a given year. GDP

Table 2.2 Types of income

Economic resource	Type of income	Owner
Land	Rent	Households
Labor	Wages and salaries	Households
Capital	Interest	Households
Entrepreneurship	Profit	Households

is widely reported in the NIPA, serving as a measure of the size of the economy. GDP includes the final value of goods and services. This calculation does not include the value of *intermediate goods*, the products used to produce final goods and services. The rule prevents "double counting," which overstates the value of output. As an example, suppose the production of tables, which sell for one hundred dollars. The per-unit input costs include:

- Wood ($40)
- Nails ($5)
- Varnish ($10)
- Box for shipping ($20)

The final price includes a per-unit markup of twenty-five dollars. But the sale increases GDP by one hundred dollars, not one hundred and seventy-five dollars ($40 + $5 + $10 + $20 + $100). The sales price includes the value of the wood, nails, varnish, box, and labor services. The latter is included in the markup.

A difference exists between the intermediate goods and physical capital. The wood, nails, varnish, and box for shipping serve as intermediate goods. During production, they are used up. But the physical capital—drill, hammer, measuring tape, saw, and screwdriver—are not used up. Over time, the physical capital loses value.

To count the value of the table, economists use the *value-added* method, which calculates the difference between the value of the final product and the cost of the intermediate goods. The producer purchases the intermediate goods from other firms.

To make the calculation, economists subtract the intermediate goods at each stage of production. In the example, the manufacturer purchases the wood, nails, varnish, and box. Including the value of the final product in GDP, and not the intermediate goods, avoids double counting.

GDP includes the production of output from all firms in the country, even if the firms are owned by foreign nationals. As long as the output is produced within the country's borders, it is included in GDP. But GDP does not include the goods and services produced by firms abroad, even if the production comes from domestic companies.

The calculation of GDP entails the application of market values for final goods and services. Even if firms produce and sell output at a loss, the final sales price serves as the unit of measurement. Economists do not use the original retail price or production cost.

GDP includes the value of legal market activity. GDP excludes output in illegal markets. In addition, GDP excludes economic activity without a market price. An example is childcare. If parents hire a nanny to take care of the children, the nanny's childcare service counts in GDP. But if the parents take care of the children themselves, the service is not counted in GDP. Therefore, GDP undercounts the value of all economic activity. To calculate GDP in the aggregate, economists use the spending and income approaches.

SPENDING APPROACH

With the spending approach, economists add up the aggregate spending on domestic goods and services. This method counts the value of sales to final buyers. The equation for GDP establishes four areas of aggregate spending:

$$GDP = C + I + G + (X - M),$$

where C is *personal consumption expenditure*, I is *gross private domestic investment*, G is *government purchases*, and $(X - M)$ is *net exports* or exports minus imports. These components represent the household, business, government, and foreign sectors.

Personal consumption expenditure includes the goods and services purchased by households and businesses. The three main categories—durables, non-durables, and services—differ with respect to their composition. Durables such as home appliances and vehicles do not wear out in a short period of time. Non-durables such as food and drinks are consumed in the present and quickly lose their value. Services, for example, in barber shops or repair shops, cannot be stored over time, but exist as specific forms of work.

Gross private domestic investment includes several categories. First, it includes the spending by firms on capital goods, such as machines, equipment, and computer systems. Second, it includes the investment in residential and nonresidential structures. Examples include the country's housing starts, hotels, motels, and manufacturing plants. Third, it includes an economic indicator, the change in business inventories:

- A rising level of inventory signals a decrease in sales, overproduction, or a forecast for a future increase in demand
- A falling level of inventory signals an increase in sales, underproduction, or a forecast for a future decrease in demand

In the process of making, providing, and selling goods and services, physical capital is an important factor of production. The *stock of capital* is the total collection of machines, equipment, and other assets that firms use to produce output. When firms acquire physical capital, gross investment occurs. But the economy will not produce as much output unless it maintains the stock of capital. In the current year, *capital depreciation* is the value of physical capital used up.

- When gross investment > capital depreciation, the stock of capital is positive
- When gross investment < capital depreciation, the stock of capital is negative

In the first case, the economy is investing in the future. In the second case, a decline in the stock of physical capital means the economy may experience a decrease in productivity.

Government purchases include the direct spending by the government at the federal, state, and local levels. The spending includes the wages and salaries of government employees. It also includes spending on defense, education, infrastructure, research and development, social programs, and transportation. Examples are spending on highway maintenance, military equipment, and office supplies for government agencies.

Net exports entail the difference between the output sold to economic agents in foreign countries and the foreign products that are imported. The spending on imports does not flow to domestic producers. As a result, imports are subtracted from GDP. In the current period, a country's *trade balance* is the difference between the market value of exports and imports:

- When exports > imports, a *trade surplus* exists
- When exports < imports, a *trade deficit* exists

Since the 1970s, the US has experienced an annual trade deficit. In the foreign sector, more money flows outside of the country than into the country.

The relative contributions of the household, business, government, and foreign sectors depend on the country. In the US, household consumption serves as the largest component, followed by business investment, government purchases, and net exports.

INCOME APPROACH

In the circular flow of economic activity, the spending that contributes to GDP establishes a flow of income. The income approach involves adding up the income earned by the factors of production. The income includes rental income, the compensation of employees, proprietors' income, corporate profits, and net interest:

- Rental income: the rent to the economic agents who lease their land or structures, plus royalties from copyrights, patents, and the rights to natural resources
- Compensation of employees: the wages, salaries, and benefits of labor, including employer-provided pensions, group health insurance, Medicare, profit-sharing plans, Social Security, and unemployment compensation
- Proprietors' income: the income earned by sole proprietorships, partnerships, and unincorporated businesses, plus the capital consumption allowance that accounts for the capital depreciation

- Corporate profits: the income that flows to corporations, adjusted for the capital consumption allowance and the valuation of inventory
- Net interest: the difference between the interest that firms pay and the interest they receive from this country and abroad

For measurement purposes, a miscellaneous adjustment subtracts foreign income and indirect business taxes (excise and sales taxes). The factors of production do not receive these payments. By adding the income and making the adjustment, the result is *national income*, the earnings from all sources of production. In the US, the payments to employees constitute the largest share of national income, followed by corporate profits, proprietors' income, rental income, and interest.

As economic agents generate GDP, they use up a portion of the economy's physical capital, including machines and equipment. If the economy produces at the same level, it must replace the physical capital. *Net domestic product* (NDP) represents the value of final goods and services in the economy, minus capital depreciation. NDP exists as the economy's output adjusted for the physical capital used up:

$$NDP = GDP - \text{capital depreciation}$$

Indirect business taxes such as sales taxes do not flow to economic agents as income, but are a part of the price of output. To calculate national income, economists subtract capital depreciation and indirect business taxes from GDP.

Personal income (Y) is the total income of households, including wages, salaries, and all labor income; dividend income; personal interest; proprietors' income; rental income; and *transfer payments*, the redistribution of income or wealth by government to qualified individuals. Transfers include Social Security and other payments. Households divide their income into *disposable income* (DI) and taxes (T):

$$Y = DI + T$$

Households then allocate DI for consumption (C) and saving (S):

$$DI = C + S$$

Households use DI to purchase financial investments (stocks, bonds, mutual funds), luxury items, and necessities. By measuring trends in consumer spending, saving, and other variables, DI serves as an indicator of the economy's strength. Economists use DI to derive discretionary income, the savings rate, and the proportion of additional income allocated to spending.

AGGREGATE OUTPUT

As this chapter explains, GDP is the economic value of final goods and services. The calculation of *nominal GDP* requires the multiplication of the quantity of output by the prices of output. Nominal GDP is useful to measure the size of the economy. But the variable is not adjusted for price-level changes. Nominal GDP increases when prices rise, even if production remains the same. But GDP is meant to measure changes in the production of output.

To account for this reality, a modified version adjusts GDP for price changes. *Real GDP* is the value of final goods and services produced in an economy in a given year, measured in constant prices. The latter means the prices in a "base year" or a starting point. With real GDP, the idea is to measure how the production of output changes over time, keeping the prices of goods and services constant.

Suppose a simple economy produces bananas and strawberries (Table 2.3). Over a two-year period, the production of output remains the same. But the per-unit prices double. In nominal terms, GDP doubles. In real terms, GDP remains the same. The

Table 2.3 Production and prices in a simple economy

	Year 1	Year 2
Quantity of bananas (millions)	100	100
Per-unit price of bananas	$0.50	$1.00
Quantity of strawberries (millions)	150	150
Per-unit price of strawberries	$1.00	$2.00
Nominal GDP (millions of dollars)	$200	$400
Real GDP (millions of year 1 dollars)	$200	$200

reason is twofold: the production of bananas and strawberries remains constant; and the simple economy counts real GDP using prices in the base period, which is year 1.

Both nominal and real GDP measure aggregate output. All else equal, larger countries have higher levels of real GDP because they have more economic resources, including the number of workers. When economists want to compare countries, they use *real GDP per capita*. This calculation eliminates the difference in population size between countries. The measure is calculated by dividing real GDP by a country's population.

Real GDP per capita measures productivity: the average amount of output per person. If real GDP per capita rises, the country's production possibility curve shifts out. The economy has more productive capacity. As a result, the economy has the potential to increase the standard of living of the country's inhabitants.

But real GDP per capita is not an equivalent to the *quality of life* or human well-being, measured by the position of individuals in society. Quality of life includes economic factors such as employment, income, and wealth. But it also includes the opportunity for education, healthcare, political representation, and social belonging. Even though the growth in real GDP per capita serves as a goal, economists do not believe that it should be the only goal. An improvement in human well-being exists as an important objective.

KEY TERMS

business cycle
capital depreciation
circular flow of economic activity
disposable income
factor markets
government purchases
Gross Domestic Product
gross private domestic investment
intermediate goods
national income
national income accounts
net domestic product
net exports

nominal GDP
personal consumption expenditure
product markets
quality of life
real GDP
real GDP per capita
recessions
stock of capital
trade balance
trade deficit
trade surplus
transfer payments

FURTHER READING

Kaminitz, Shiri. 2023. "The significance of GDP: a new take on a century-old question." *Journal of Economic Methodology*, 30 (1): 1–14.

Lainé, Michael. 2018. "The Confidence Paradox: Can Confidence Account for Business Cycles?" *Journal of Economic Issues*, 52 (1): 136–156.

Zink, Trevor and Geyer, Roland. 2017. "Circular Economy Rebound." *Journal of Industrial Ecology*, 21 (3): 593–602.

3

UNEMPLOYMENT

UNEMPLOYMENT DURING THE PANDEMIC

In 2020, at the onset of the coronavirus pandemic, the government of the United States (US) implemented non-pharmaceutical interventions to slow the spread of the pathogen. Many businesses closed. Face-to-face meetings switched to an online format. Commuters avoided buses, trains, and vehicles, shifting their labor efforts to the home environment. These policy interventions impacted the *labor market*, which includes the individuals who supply their labor services and the businesses that hire workers. Fewer individuals returned to the office. Businesses produced less output, leading to a decrease in the demand for labor. During the early months of the pandemic, the *labor force* shrank. The labor force includes the people in the economy who are working or actively seeking jobs.

These forces altered the *unemployment rate*, which is calculated by dividing the number of people who are unemployed by the labor force:

$$\text{Unemployment rate} = \text{number of people unemployed}/\text{labor force}$$

According to the US Bureau of Labor Statistics (BLS), in February 2020, the unemployment rate was 3.5 percent. But by April 2020, the US unemployment rate increased to 14.8 percent. The change existed as an unusual spike in the unemployment rate (Figure 3.1).

DOI: 10.4324/9781003678700-4

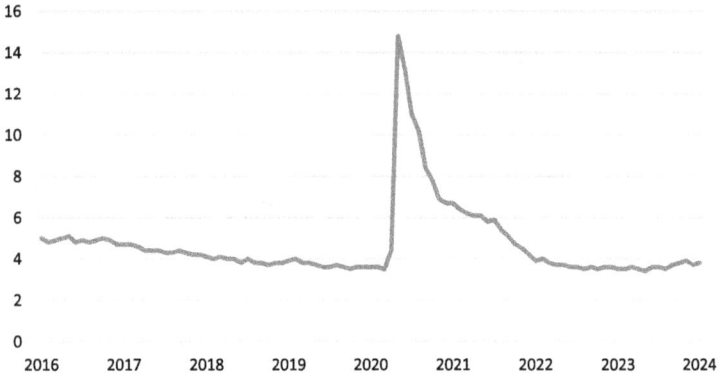

Figure 3.1 Unemployment rate in the US (%)
Source: Author using data from the US Bureau of Labor Statistics, https://data.
bls.gov/timeseries/LNS14000000

Even though the pandemic impacted the economy through a number of pathways, including the product and factor markets, the decrease in consumer demand led to a decrease in the demand for labor. In addition, government shutdowns reduced the density of workers in the economy, decreasing labor supply. Before the process of economic recovery began, at the end of 2020, millions of people lost their jobs. Because of the large and sudden increase in the unemployment rate, this outcome was unusual.

Not including the pandemic year of 2020, the unemployment rate of the US fluctuated during 2014–2024, from a low of 3.5 percent in July 2022 to a high of 6.7 percent in February 2014. This band represents a strong economy over a ten-year period of time with the exception of 2020 when the pandemic shut down many sectors of the economy.

The fact that the post-pandemic economy in 2023–2024 was characterized by unemployment rates below 4.3 percent signified a rapid recovery. The reasons for the rapid recovery were a rapid deployment of vaccines, strong support from the federal government, and the economy's ability to withstand the external shock.

Another method to assess labor market trends is the *employment-to-population ratio*. The ratio is the percentage of the population that is employed:

Employment-to-population ratio = number of people
employed/population

A rising ratio signifies an economic expansion, when more
people are employed. A falling ratio signifies an economic contraction, when fewer people are employed. Economists use the
ratio as a method to evaluate the health of the economy. But
economists may also use the ratio to evaluate employment trends
by ethnicity, gender, and race. In the US, the ratio indicates the
impact of the coronavirus pandemic (Figure 3.2).

Evaluating the ratio over time demonstrates the extreme change
during 2020. From 2016 to the end of 2019, the ratio fluctuated
between 59.7 percent in January 2016 and 61.1 percent in
December 2019. But the pandemic caused the ratio to fall to as
low as 51.2 percent in April 2020. This minimum point served as
an important metric. The population remained relatively constant,
but the number of people employed decreased.

While the unemployment rate and employment-to-population
ratio are both useful to assess the strength of the economy, they
assess different parts of the population. The unemployment rate
uses the size of the labor force as its point of reference. The labor

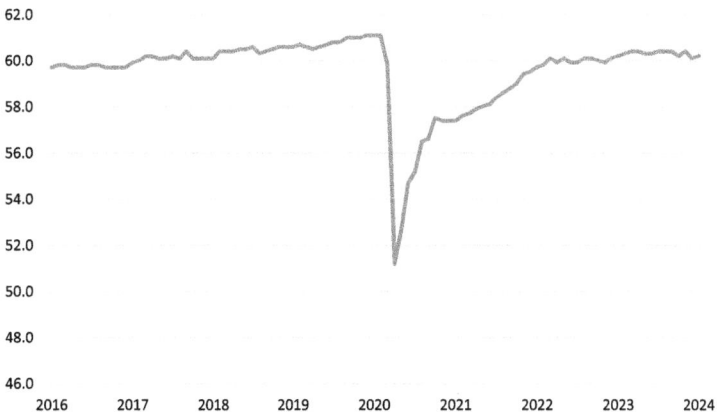

Figure 3.2 Employment-to-population ratio in the US (%)
Source: Author using data from the Federal Reserve Bank, https://fred.
stlouisfed.org/series/EMRATIO

force includes working members of the population and those who are actively seeking employment, but it excludes the individuals who are not actively seeking work. Therefore, the labor force is less than the population, the latter serving as the point of reference for the employment-to-population ratio.

In macroeconomics, the unemployment rate serves as an important economic indicator. When people are unemployed, they lose their wages or salaries, and the economy loses the output they would have produced. A decrease in consumer spending from the rise in the unemployment rate leads to a multiplier effect, creating an economic context in which other workers may lose their jobs. Because the unemployment rate serves as an important macroeconomic indicator, the chapter explains how economists define and measure unemployment, how unemployment impacts the economy, and the pattern of employment changes.

DEFINING AND MEASURING UNEMPLOYMENT

In the US, the BLS publishes three main monthly statistics: the number of people employed, the number of people unemployed, and the size of the labor force. Economists use these statistics to determine the unemployment rate, employment-to-population ratio, and other statistics. For the people who are employed, the BLS counts individuals who have worked for pay or profit during the survey period. Employment includes the individuals with full-time, part-time, or temporary work. The BLS considers individuals unemployed if they do not have work but are available for work and are actively seeking employment for the four weeks preceding the employment survey. Actively seeking work includes activities such as contacting employment agencies, responding to ads for employment, scheduling interviews, sending resumes, and visiting placement centers.

EMPLOYMENT SURVEYS

In the US, both the Department of Labor and Census Bureau survey households, firms, and government agencies to determine changes in employment. The payroll survey of the Department of Labor determines the number of employees working for 400,000 firms and government agencies. If the number of jobs changes, the survey reveals the increase or decrease. With the household survey, the Census Bureau contacts 60,000 households in 700 geographical areas to determine their employment status. Representing the entire population, the survey asks individuals about their full-time work, part-time work, unpaid family work, agricultural work, household work, and other forms of employment. With the information, the Bureau determines the number of individuals who are employed, unemployed, or not in the labor force.

Because the surveys provide monthly data, they determine the economy's employment trends. The payroll survey reveals the changes in nonfarm payroll employment, focusing on the economy's industries and regions. The household survey reveals a broader picture of the labor market, including entrepreneurial activity, the self-employed, and the individuals working in agriculture. Because the payroll survey is larger, macroeconomists view it as a more accurate representation of economic activity. But both of the surveys provide valuable information.

According to the data, in December 2024, in the US, 161 million people were employed, 7 million were unemployed, and 101 million were not in the labor force (Figure 3.3). To calculate the unemployment rate, the 7 million unemployed divided by the 161 million in the labor force equals 0.041 or a 4.1 percent unemployment rate.

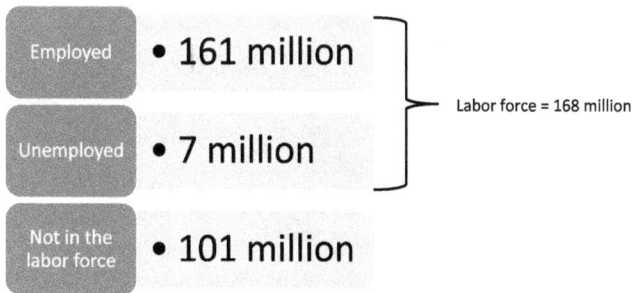

Figure 3.3 Employment, unemployment, and the labor force in the US, December 2024

Source: US Bureau of Labor Statistics, https://www.bls.gov/news.release/emp sit.nr0.htm

LABOR FORCE PARTICIPATION

While the labor force includes the individuals who are employed or unemployed, cycling may occur between the two positions. Individuals who accelerate their movement to retirement exit the labor force. During uncertain periods, some members of the labor force may leave their jobs. The *labor force participation rate* provides the percentage of individuals of the working age population who have employment or are actively seeking jobs:

$$\text{Labor force participation rate} = \text{labor force/working-age population}$$

The labor force participation rate demonstrates when economic conditions alter the supply of labor (Figure 3.4). Several factors impact the rate, including an economy that encourages employment, job opportunities in the labor market, policies for education and training, the size of the working-age population, and external shocks. When the rate is relatively high, a robust economy is creating jobs, individuals are seeking work, and a healthy labor market provides positions for the individuals entering the labor force.

Figure 3.4 Labor force participation rate in the US (%)
Source: Author using data from the Federal Reserve Bank, https://fred.stlouisfed.org/series/CIVPART

In 2020, during the coronavirus pandemic, when schools and day care centers shut down, many people had to leave their jobs to care for their children. The labor force participation rate plummeted.

EMPLOYMENT AND UNEMPLOYMENT

With the calculation of the unemployment rate, the labor force serves as an important factor. In the US, the labor force increases on an annual basis by one million or more workers. Because the country's annual fertility rate is at or below the rate of replacement, the increase in population is due to immigration. When the population increases, the labor force increases. To maintain the unemployment rate, the economy has to create enough jobs to keep pace with the increase in the labor force.

The unemployment rate may not demonstrate a negative correlation with employment. The number of people employed may increase at the same time that the unemployment rate rises. The reason is the labor force could increase more than employment.

The payroll and household surveys that estimate employment, unemployment, and the size of the labor force are not exact measures. For many reasons, people enter and exit the labor force, which complicates the determination of their employment status. The reasons include college, external factors, family matters, and retirement. As a result, the surveys may not identify individual workers who move into and out of the labor force.

In particular, the surveys struggle to identify chronically underemployed individuals who are discouraged and frustrated with their job opportunities. Because they cannot find suitable forms of employment, they drop out of the labor force. Economists acknowledge that the unemployment rate does not capture these individuals: because they are not actively seeking employment, they are not a part of the labor force. A *discouraged worker* does not actively look for a job but prefers to work.

Several reasons exist for discouraged workers. They may not have the appropriate education, skills, or training. They may not be able to find work in their area, but cannot move. They may not have the confidence to apply for jobs. They may experience poverty and discrimination. Other reasons may exist. The point is that discouraged workers are marginally attached to the labor force and are available to work, but they have not looked for work in the four weeks before the employment survey. As a result, the survey does not see them as part of the labor force. During the contractionary phase of the business cycle, employment opportunities decrease. During this time, the number of discouraged workers increases.

Overall, the measurement of employment and unemployment statistics depends on the applications of the data. Economists use the information to assess the state of the economy, evaluate the distribution of unemployment, and estimate the extent to which individuals lack sufficient work opportunities.

The BLS publishes data on one more important variable: *underemployment*, when the positions of individuals do not utilize their education, experience, or skills. This concept also applies to part-time employees who want to work full time.

As a measure of the labor market conditions, underemployment signals the divergence between labor supply and labor demand. If the economy sorts the members of the labor force into their jobs, the workers are using their skill sets. But a rise in underemployment stems from advances in technology, competition in the job market, the contractionary phase of the business cycle, limited employment opportunities, and a lack of fit between the job requirements and the skills of workers. For the individuals who are underemployed, the problem may have long-term consequences, such as financial instability, a loss of confidence, and lower job satisfaction.

UNEMPLOYMENT AND THE ECONOMY

During each phase of the business cycle, the economy experiences unemployment. The unemployment rate never reaches zero percent, even when the economy is booming. If the wages of specific jobs are set above the equilibrium rate, unemployment may persist. Both union bargaining and minimum wages create this divergence. For the individuals who have unionized or entry-level jobs, their earnings rise. But unions and minimum wages restrict the employment of some people who are willing and able to work. In these contexts, employers offer wages that are above the equilibrium rate (*efficiency wages*) in order to boost worker morale, increase labor productivity, or maintain a stable set of employees. But these wages prevent firms from hiring additional workers, contributing to the unemployment rate. Overall, different types of unemployment exist.

TYPES OF UNEMPLOYMENT

Cyclical unemployment results from the contractionary phase of the business cycle. When economic growth occurs, firms produce more output and demand more workers. But in an economic contraction, firms produce less. As their inventory rises, they lay off workers. As individuals lose their jobs, cyclical unemployment becomes a negative factor for the economy.

Frictional unemployment results from the time that individuals spend looking for work. If all forms of employment and workers were alike, job searches would proceed in a straightforward manner. If the job market information were available to everyone, the labor market would efficiently sort those looking for jobs into available positions. But individuals entering the labor force may struggle to find their first employment opportunities. Other individuals who have been working may decide to switch jobs or careers. For some workers, it takes time to find jobs that are good fits for their abilities, personalities, and expertise. Finding the proper information about employment opportunities may complicate the process. It is normal for those looking for work to spend a few weeks in the process. As a result, a certain amount of frictional unemployment will always exist.

Structural unemployment occurs when there are more people seeking jobs in a specific labor market than there are jobs available. This form of unemployment may exist at any point in the business cycle. The reason is the change in consumer demand or technology. When industries change, the individuals available for work may have specific skills. But the employers may not demand the skill sets. When products or industries become obsolete, the skills honed by the workers in the industries become obsolete. Examples include the individuals who work in manufacturing, but the jobs leave for another region; or individuals who obtain the skills to work in a specific industry, but the industry downsizes. Whereas frictional unemployment is normally short-term, structural unemployment occurs over longer periods of time.

NATURAL RATE OF UNEMPLOYMENT

In addition to using changes in GDP to measure the health of the economy, economists look to the unemployment rate. In particular, they compare the actual unemployment rate to full employment, which occurs when the economy is employing all of its economic resources. In the field of macroeconomics, full employment is equivalent to the *natural rate of unemployment*, when unemployment is frictional and structural, but cyclical is equal to zero. In this context, a certain amount of unemployment is "natural," or always exists. The natural rate of unemployment is the rate at which the actual unemployment rate fluctuates. When they are equal, the economy is operating as efficiently and productively as it can.

With these concepts, a more technical way to define cyclical unemployment is the difference between the actual unemployment rate and the natural rate. The natural rate of unemployment serves as an important policy variable, helping both economists and policy makers to assess the relative strength of the economy. What is the specific estimate? In the US, in 2020, economists estimated the natural rate of unemployment to equal 5 percent. To make forecasts, economists working for firms and the government needed the estimate. In sum:

Natural unemployment = frictional unemployment + structural unemployment

Actual unemployment = natural unemployment + cyclical unemployment

The natural rate of unemployment does not remain constant. Over time, changes occur. The reasons include changes in government policies, labor force characteristics, and labor market institutions. First, government policies such as more generous employment benefits or an increase in the minimum wage contribute to both frictional and structural unemployment, increasing the natural rate of unemployment. These policies complicate the process of finding a job and establish a shortage of workers at the prevailing wage. But job training programs and employment subsidies (payments to employers or workers) decrease the natural rate of unemployment. Second, changes in labor force characteristics reflect a dynamic labor market. Older and more experienced workers have lower levels of frictional unemployment. They tend to stay in their jobs longer. They have an easier time finding new forms of unemployment. They have a greater incentive to seek stable forms of employment. As a result, as the labor force is more experienced, the natural rate of unemployment declines. Third, changes in labor market institutions, such as labor unions, impact the natural rate of unemployment. Strong labor unions restrict the number of workers in unionized industries, increasing the natural rate of unemployment. But employment agencies decrease frictional unemployment and the natural rate by matching workers with job.

REASONS FOR STRUCTURAL UNEMPLOYMENT

In most markets, the prices adjust to find an equilibrium between the quantity demanded and the quantity supplied. In these situations, the equilibrium serves as a market-clearing point. As this chapter explains, the labor market includes the supply of labor by individuals and the demand for labor by firms. In an efficient labor market, the wage adjusts so that the quantity of labor supplied equals the quantity of labor demanded. But the types of unemployment make clear that there are always some workers without jobs. The unemployment rate never equals zero. In contrast, the actual unemployment rate fluctuates around the natural rate. The frictional unemployment during shorter periods of time occurs when the labor market is slow to match workers with jobs.

But the structural unemployment that lasts for longer periods occurs when the actual wage (w) for specific jobs exceeds the equilibrium wage (w_e). At the higher wage, the quantity of labor supplied (Q_S) is greater than the quantity of labor demanded (Q_D). A surplus of labor exists (Figure 3.5). Because economies often struggle with structural unemployment, the following sections discuss the reasons for the problem.

EFFICIENCY WAGES

The first reason that structural unemployment exists is the efficiency wages that some firms pay to workers. According to the theory of efficiency wages, firms operate more efficiently if the wage paid to

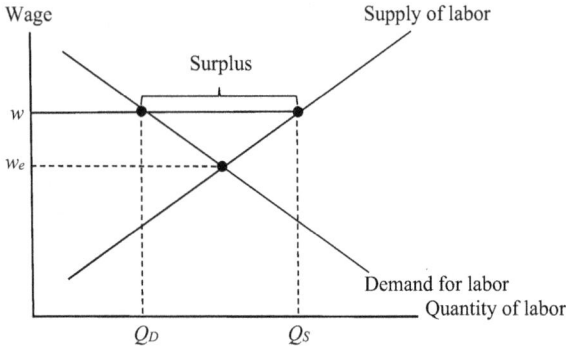

Figure 3.5 Surplus of labor in the labor market

employees exceeds the equilibrium wage. The workers are more productive. But the choice entails costs and benefits. Because labor serves as a cost of production, the higher wages increase production costs. Economists identify profit maximization as the objective of firms. All else equal, higher costs lead to lower profits. But the theory of efficiency wages implies that the higher wage increases worker productivity, output, revenue, and profit.

Four types of efficiency wages exist. First, when workers are paid higher wages, they experience healthier lifestyles, increasing productivity. Second, higher wages reduce worker turnover. Third, when firms pay higher wages, they attract a more talented pool of workers. Fourth, higher wages inspire workers to try harder in the production process.

Together, the types of efficiency wages explain why many firms are reluctant to cut wages, even during economic contractions. Firms find it profitable to pay workers w instead of w_e because the premium attracts higher-quality workers, lowers worker malfeasance, reduces turnover, and facilitates productivity.

FUNDAMENTAL CHANGES IN THE ECONOMY

The second reason that structural unemployment exists is fundamental changes in the economy. These changes include globalization, industry decline, shifts in consumer preferences, and technological advancements.

- Globalization means the increasing level of interconnection between countries, companies, and individuals. With this process occurring on a global scale, it is easier for firms to relocate their production to the most cost-effective areas of the world. The workers in the areas that are left behind experience structural unemployment.

- Industry decline results from changing market forces or conditions, such as external shocks, financial instability, or trade barriers. The workers who do not have the skills to operate in different economic environments are structurally unemployed.

- Changes in consumer preferences may lead to a decrease in demand for specific goods and services. Examples include a shift to online shopping rather than shopping in a mall, a focus on social responsibility rather than products that come from polluting industries, and subscription-based entertainment rather than cable. If workers do not have the skills to transition to other industries, structural unemployment increases.

- When technological advancements such as artificial intelligence replace laborers, specific jobs become obsolete. Examples include work in computer programming, customer service, graphic design, paralegal, and research. To remain employed, the displaced workers must obtain new skills.

LABOR UNIONS

The third reason that structural unemployment exists is labor unions and collective bargaining. *Labor unions* are associations or groups of people with a common interest or purpose. By negotiating better working conditions, labor unions improve the economic conditions of their members. Labor unions promote their interests in different ways, including better benefits, higher salaries, and workplace safety. The process of *collective bargaining* exists as a form of negotiation between labor unions and employers. It establishes a contract that governs the terms and conditions of employment. But to maintain strength in the bargaining process, labor unions control the supply of labor in the industry. This process increases bargaining power and wages, but decreases the number of workers employed. As a result, more individuals are willing to work at the higher wage. But if employers are less likely to hire, a mismatch exists between the skills of the workers and the number of available jobs, a contribution to structural unemployment.

MINIMUM WAGES

The fourth reason that structural unemployment exists is the existence of minimum wages. Many countries around the world have passed a minimum wage law. As opposed to labor unions, the minimum wage is intended to help young workers and the individuals at the bottom of the socioeconomic ladder.

The law sets a floor price in the labor market for entry-level jobs. Because the market establishes an equilibrium wage that society considers to be too low, the law raises the wage that firms must pay. In the US, the federal government sets a national minimum wage, but states may raise it. The minimum wage helps the workers to afford basic necessities, such as food, clothing, and shelter.

For a minimum wage to be effective, the government sets it above the equilibrium wage. But the establishment of a minimum wage creates a tradeoff. For the workers, the higher wage helps entry-level workers consume more goods and services. But it may cause firms to hire fewer employees.

The reason is that firms hire additional workers if they think the workers will add more value than what they cost. The difference flows to the firms in the form of profit. As a result, a minimum wage increases living standards for those who have jobs. But it may complicate the process of finding employment. Even though the minimum wage is not a major reason for unemployment, it impacts certain groups within the economy. Referring to Figure 3.5, if the minimum wage is set at w, it leads to a surplus of labor by the difference between Q_S and Q_D. The surplus exists as a form of structural unemployment.

According to economic theory, the outcome is mixed. Most workers make more than the minimum wage. As a result, they are not impacted by the resulting unemployment. But if the minimum wage decreases the quantity demanded of labor below the equilibrium point, young and unskilled workers may struggle to acquire the experience and skills necessary to find higher paying jobs.

What does the research on the minimum wage conclude? Some studies find that the minimum wage contributes to structural unemployment. But other studies show that the law has little impact on unemployment. Firms may compensate for the higher wage by increasing the performance standards of workers. To offset the higher labor cost, the employees have to be more productive. Firms may discourage overtime work or pass on the cost to customers in the form of higher prices. In practice, firms often find other ways to account for the minimum wage, rather than cutting jobs. Given the mixed results from this research, economic theory suggests that the minimum wage contributes to structural unemployment among young and unskilled workers.

KEY TERMS

collective bargaining
cyclical unemployment
discouraged worker
efficiency wages
employment-to-population ratio
frictional unemployment
labor force
labor force participation rate
labor market
labor unions
natural rate of unemployment
structural unemployment
underemployment
unemployment rate

FURTHER READING

Albanesi, Stefania and Kim, Jiyeon. 2021. "Effects of the Covid-19 Recession on the US Labor Market: Occupation, Family, and Gender." *Journal of Economic Perspectives*, 35 (3): 3–24.

Bhuller, Manudeep, Moene, Karl, Mogstad, Magne and Vestad, Ola. 2022. "Facts and Fantasies about Wage Setting and Collective Bargaining." *Journal of Economic Perspectives*, 36 (4): 29–52.

Manning, Alan. 2021. "The Elusive Employment Effect of the Minimum Wage." *Journal of Economic Perspectives*, 35 (1): 3–26.

4

INFLATION

INFLATION DURING THE PANDEMIC

The coronavirus pandemic disrupted economic activity. During 2020, the economy of the United States (US) lost over 20 million jobs, leading to an economic contraction. In response, the federal government increased the amount of aid flowing to households. At the same time, the central bank increased the money supply, decreasing both interest rates and borrowing costs. By the end of 2020, the economy began to recover. Consumer spending increased. Businesses hired workers. But a problem emerged: *inflation*, a general increase in the price level. The rising inflation rate impacted the macroeconomy, including a redistribution of income and wealth.

To determine the inflation rate, the US Bureau of Labor Statistics (BLS) determines the *Consumer Price Index* (CPI), a measure of the average change in prices for goods and services. When the CPI increases, inflation occurs. When the CPI decreases, *deflation* occurs, a general decrease in the price level. In January 2021, one year into the pandemic, the CPI was 1.4 percent higher than the previous year. By historical standards, the rate was typical.

But the CPI began to rise. On the supply side of the market, global supply chain problems resulted from factory closures, labor shortages, problems in global shipping, and transportation bottlenecks. In many industries, the decrease in market supply pressured prices to increase. On the demand side of the market, federal governments, including the US, implemented expansionary fiscal policy, sending money directly to households. By the end of 2020,

DOI: 10.4324/9781003678700-5

US households accumulated more than $2 trillion dollars in savings, according to the Federal Reserve Bank. Because of government and household spending, market demand increased, putting an upward pressure on prices.

Together, the decrease in market supply and increase in market demand increased the rate of inflation. In June 2021, the inflation rate rose to 5.39 percent compared to the previous year. By June 2022, the inflation rate peaked, reaching 9.06 percent compared to the previous year. It was the highest rate in more than 40 years.

Several problems emerged. Consumer purchasing power decreased. The same amount of money bought fewer goods and services. The higher inflation rate disproportionately impacted lower-income households with fewer financial assets. Inflation expectations rose, leading to higher wages and further increases in output prices. Interest rates increased, reflecting the policy of the central bank to fight the rise in the price level. Higher borrowing costs led to a decrease in spending in the household and business sectors.

Because inflation serves as an important indicator of the health of the economy, the following sections discuss the causes of inflation, measurement of inflation, other price measures, the costs of inflation, inflation expectations, and redistributive effects.

CAUSES OF INFLATION

A general increase in prices requires an explanation. What causes this outcome to occur? The reason is a change in market conditions. On the demand side, excessive spending puts an upward pressure on prices. If there is an increase in household consumption, business investment, government expenditure, and demand for exports, the market demand for output rises. In this case, the demand may exceed the ability of the economy to produce goods and services, creating the classic case of "too much money chasing too few goods." As inventory declines, prices rise. When an increase in market demand leads to higher prices, *demand-pull inflation* occurs. On the supply side, an increase in the prices of goods and services results from a decrease in market supply. During the pandemic, this outcome resulted from the global supply chain shortage. But a decrease in market supply also results from an increase in the cost of economic resources, a decline in the availability of labor and capital, and higher cost of energy and raw materials. When a decrease in market supply leads to higher prices, *cost-push inflation* exists.

MEASURING INFLATION

Just as macroeconomists use a statistic to measure the overall level of output (GDP), they use a statistic to measure the overall level of prices: the *aggregate price level*. But consumers purchase thousands of goods and services. How do economists determine the aggregate price level? They use a *price index*, which is the weighted average of prices for a set of goods and services. For the general population, the price index represents a key indicator of the cost of living. To determine the price index, economists evaluate consumer spending in a basket of goods and services.

MARKET BASKET

The CPI uses a market basket to track changes in the price level. The market basket includes the items that urban consumers normally buy. It is a fixed set of items that reflects their consumption habits. The CPI's market basket includes several major categories, such as apparel, education and communication, food and beverages, housing, medical care, and recreation. But the BLS collects price data in these categories for thousands of items, representing a large sample. Each item receives an item weight, equal to the typical spending proportion by consumers. Consumers spend a large percentage of their budgets on energy, food, and housing. When the prices of these items rise, the impact on the CPI is more significant than for the products with low item weights.

ITEM WEIGHT AND INFLATION

To demonstrate the concept of item weight, suppose a simplified example of spending by a college student. Each week, the student spends money on pizza, ramen, drinks, and apples (Table 4.1). Given the per-unit prices, the student spends $105.00 on pizza, $7.00 on ramen, $42.00 on drinks, and $6.00 on apples for a total of $160.00.

Table 4.1 Hypothetical consumption budget

	Pizza	Ramen	Drinks	Apples	Total
Quantity demanded	7	14	21	6	
Price	$15.00	$0.50	$2.00	$1.00	
Spending	$105.00	$7.00	$42.00	$6.00	$160.00
Formula for item weight	$105.00 ÷ $160.00	$7.00 ÷ $160.00	$42.00 ÷ $160.00	$6.00 ÷ $160.00	
Item weight	0.65625	0.04375	0.2625	0.0375	1

The item weight equals the spending on the item divided by total spending. For example, the item weights for pizza and ramen are:

$$Item\ weight_{pizza} = \frac{spending\ on\ pizza}{total\ spending} = \frac{\$105.00}{\$160.00} = 0.65625$$

$$Item\ weight_{ramen} = \frac{spending\ on\ ramen}{total\ spending} = \frac{\$7.00}{\$160.00} = 0.04375$$

The calculations reveal that the student spends 65.625 percent of the total budget on pizza and 4.375 percent of the total budget on ramen. In this market basket, an increase in the price of pizza carries a greater weight than an increase in the price of ramen. In the table, adding each item weight yields the total of one. To calculate the overall inflation impact, the CPI holds each item weight constant. Suppose the price of each item increases by the following percentages:

- pizza (20 percent)
- ramen (25 percent)
- drinks (30 percent)
- apples (35 percent)

For each item, the increase in price leads to a decrease in the quantity demanded, reflecting the Law of Demand (Table 4.2). For example, the quantity demanded for pizza decreases from 7

Table 4.2 Inflation impact

	Pizza	*Ramen*	*Drinks*	*Apples*	*Total*
New quantity demanded	6	12	20	5	
Old price	$15.00	$0.50	$2.00	$1.00	
Price increase	20%	25%	30%	35%	
New price	$18.00	$0.625	$2.60	$1.35	
Spending	$108.00	$7.50	$52.00	$6.75	$174.25
Item weight (constant)	0.65625	0.04375	0.2625	0.0375	1
Inflation impact	0.13125	0.0109375	0.07875	0.013125	0.2340625

pizzas to 6 pizzas. The quantity demanded of ramen decreases from 14 units to 12 units. After the increase in price and decrease in quantity demanded, the total spending of the student rises from $160.00 to $174.25.

For each product, the inflation impact equals the increase in price times the item weight, which remains constant. For pizza and ramen, the inflation impacts are:

$$Inflation\,impact_{pizza} = (increase\,in\,price)\,(item\,weight)$$

$$= (0.20)\,(0.65625) = 0.13125$$

$$Inflation\,impact_{ramen} = (increase\,in\,price)\,(item\,weight)$$

$$= (0.25)\,(0.04375) = 0.0109375$$

In the example, the prices increase by different percentages. As a result, each item has a different inflation impact, demonstrated by the numbers in the bottom row in Table 4.2. The overall increase in the price level of 23.40625 percent is calculated by adding the inflation impact of each item. Of the total inflation impact, pizza contributes the most (13.125 percent), followed by drinks (7.875 percent), apples (1.3125 percent), and ramen (1.09375 percent). The outcome reflects the relative weights of importance of each item.

USES OF THE CPI DATA

In the US, the CPI serves as the most widely used price index. The CPI demonstrates how the cost of items in the market basket changes over time, compared to a *base period*. The base period serves as a point of reference, currently equal to 100 in 1982–1984. For example, according to the BLS, in December 2024, the CPI was equal to 315. This means that, compared to the base period, the price level increased by 215 percent. During this century, the CPI demonstrates a general increase in the price level (Figure 4.1).

By using the CPI, economists calculate an important macro-economic indicator: the *inflation rate*. The inflation rate is the annual percentage change in the price index:

$$Inflation\, rate = \frac{price\, index\, in\, year\, 2 - price\, index\, in\, year\, 1}{price\, index\, in\, year\, 1} \times 100$$

Table 4.3 includes the values of the CPI in the US from 2001 to 2024.

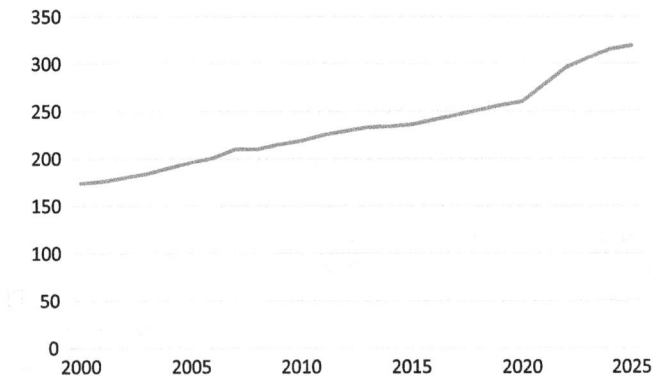

Figure 4.1 Inflation according to the CPI, 1982–1984 = 100
Source: Author using data from the US BLS, https://data.bls.gov/timeseries/CUUR0000SA0?years_option=all_years

Table 4.3 CPI in the US

Year	CPI	Year	CPI
2001	176	2013	233
2002	180	2014	234
2003	184	2015	236
2004	190	2016	241
2005	196	2017	246
2006	201	2018	251
2007	210	2019	256
2008	210	2020	260
2009	215	2021	278
2010	219	2022	296
2011	225	2023	306
2012	229	2024	315

Source: US BLS, https://data.bls.gov/timeseries/CUUR0000SA0?years_option=all_years

Using the CPI data, the inflation rates for 2022 and 2024 are:

$$Inflation\,rate_{2022} = \frac{296 - 278}{278} \times 100 = 0.065 \times 100 = 6.5\%$$

$$Inflation\,rate_{2024} = \frac{315 - 306}{306} \times 100 = 0.029 \times 100 = 2.9\%$$

Relative to the high inflation rate in 2022, the inflation rate in 2024 was closer to the average rate in the US of 2.5 percent during the first two and a half decades of this century.

CORE INFLATION

Economists often focus on *core inflation* as the change in the cost of goods and services, excluding the energy and food sectors. The reason is that energy and food prices are more volatile. To households, energy and food are staples, meaning the demand for them changes very little when prices increase. As an example, when the global market sets a higher price for oil, the price of gasoline increases. Oil and gas are commodities. They are bought and sold in commodity exchanges. The speculation that exists in the exchanges leads to price volatility. For inflation calculations, the volatility creates sudden swings. As a result, economists exclude energy and food from the determination of core inflation.

PROTECTIVE MECHANISMS

In contrast to GDP, the CPI directly impacts the lives of consumers. Price-level changes alter purchasing power, impacting the ability of consumers to purchase goods and services. Given the causes of inflation, individuals do not want to bear the burden of higher prices. Even with a low inflation rate, the real value of money decreases. If the annual inflation rate equals 3 percent, the real value of $1,000 declines to $970.87 in one year, $942.59 in two years, and further in subsequent years.

Protective mechanisms insulate individuals from the effects of inflation. In the US, Social Security—the federal government program that provides financial protection for disabled, retired, and surviving individuals—employs a cost-of-living adjustment (COLA) to ensure that nominal benefits keep pace with the rate of inflation. The Social Security payments are adjusted annually, according to the CPI. Landlords, furthermore, often include in their contracts a provision that increases the rent according to the rate of inflation. Finally, loan agreements use COLAs. Suppose a loan requires a 2 percent interest payment on the amount of the principal borrowed. If the inflation rate equals 3 percent, the price level increases faster than the accumulation of interest. In this case, the *real interest rate*, an interest rate adjusted for the rate of inflation, is negative:

$$\text{Real interest } rate \ = \ nominal\, interest\, rate \ - \ rate\, of\, inflation$$

$$2\% \ - \ 3\% \ = \ -1\%$$

The implication is that the future interest payments will purchase fewer goods than today. For the length of the loan, if the rate of inflation exceeds the nominal interest rate, the level of real wealth of the lender decreases.

OTHER PRICE MEASURES

In addition to the CPI, economists use other measures to track price changes. The measures provide a different perspective, focusing on consumers, producers, and the production of output.

PERSONAL CONSUMPTION EXPENDITURES INDEX

The Bureau of Economic Analysis derives the *Personal Consumption Expenditures Index* (PCEI) using survey data on sales. To assess inflationary trends, the US Central Bank prioritizes the PCEI. In two ways, the PCEI differs from the CPI. First, the PCEI measures the spending by US households on all goods and services, including the expenditures made on their behalf by firms. In contrast, the CPI focuses on the out-of-pocket expenditures by households on goods and services, but excludes indirect expenditures on their behalf, including medical care payments by employers and Medicare payments by the government. The PCEI includes the latter payments. Second, the indexes differ with respect to the market basket. When prices change and consumers alter their spending habits, the market basket of the PCEI adjusts. If the price of eggs increases and the consumers substitute away to other breakfast items, the PCEI uses a different market basket, reflecting the smaller weight of eggs. In contrast, if the quantity demanded changes for specific goods and services, the CPI uses the same market basket.

PRODUCER PRICE INDEX

The *Producer Price Index* (PPI) measures the average change in the output prices received by domestic producers. For goods and services, the prices in the PPI come from the first commercial transactions. To measure the price changes, the PPI includes several categories, including construction, electricity, food and alcohol retailing, machinery and equipment, mining and manufacturing, and services. As with the CPI, the BLS publishes monthly data for the PPI. The information allows economists to monitor changes in the economy. In the index, food and energy are more volatile. In addition to a PPI index that includes all categories, economists calculate a PPI index that excludes food and energy. The latter calculation facilitates the analysis of price movements with less volatility. When the market demand for output changes, producers are quick to alter their prices. As a result, the PPI responds faster to inflationary pressures than the CPI. Economists look to an increase in the PPI as an early sign of inflation.

GDP DEFLATOR

The GDP deflator measures the change in prices of all goods and services in the economy, excluding imports. Therefore, it differs from the CPI, which measures consumer goods, and the PPI, which measures producer goods. Using a base year of 2017 equal to 100, the GDP deflator measures the extent to which inflation adjusts the value of an economy's output (Figure 4.2). Economists use the GDP deflator to measure the change in the production of output in the economy, rather than the change in the dollar value of output, which occurs when prices increase or decrease.

Economists use the GDP deflator to depict economic growth. The calculation of nominal GDP requires the prices that exist in a specific year. If the prices rise, nominal GDP increases. In this context, the change obscures the fact that production may not change. As a result, economists calculate real GDP, which is output-adjusted for inflation. Real GDP calculates the change in production, using

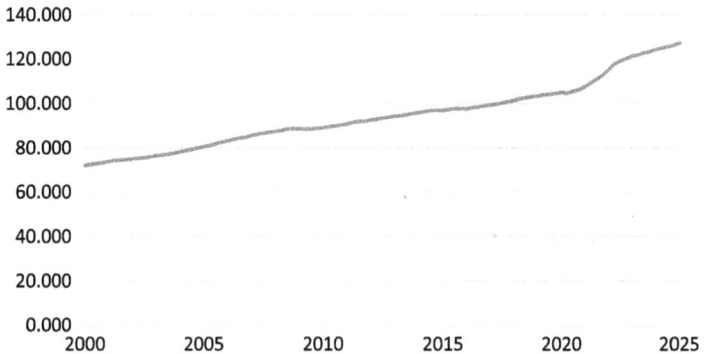

Figure 4.2 GDP deflator, 2017 = 100
Source: Author using data from the Federal Reserve Bank, https://fred. stlouisfed.org/series/GDPDEF

constant prices. In particular, real GDP equals nominal GDP divided by the GDP deflator:

$$\text{Real}\,GDP = \frac{Nominal\,GDP}{GDP\,deflator}.$$

To determine the change in production, economists extract the impact of inflation on nominal GDP. The application uses the equation to inflate or deflate the nominal value of GDP. With 2017 as the base year, Table 4.4 lists the GDP deflator, according to the Federal Reserve Bank.

Economists use the GDP deflator to solve different problems. In 2010, US nominal GDP was equal to $15,049 billion, according to the Federal Reserve Bank. To calculate real GDP in billions of 2017 dollars, nominal GDP is inflated with an alteration of the denominator. Using the GDP deflator for 2010, the calculation is:

$$Real\,GDP_{2010} = \frac{\$15,049\,billion}{90/100} = \frac{\$15,049\,billion}{0.90} = \$16,721\,billion.$$

Table 4.4 GDP deflator in the US

Year	GDP deflator	Year	GDP deflator
2001	74	2013	95
2002	76	2014	96
2003	77	2015	97
2004	79	2016	98
2005	82	2017	100
2006	84	2018	103
2007	86	2019	104
2008	88	2020	106
2009	88	2021	112
2010	90	2022	120
2011	91	2023	123
2012	93	2024	126

Source: Federal Reserve Bank, https://fred.stlouisfed.org/series/GDPDEF

In 2024, US nominal GDP was equal to \$29,167 billion, according to the Federal Reserve Bank. To calculate real GDP in billions of 2017 dollars, nominal GDP is deflated. Using the GDP deflator for 2024, the calculation is:

$$Real\,GDP_{2024} = \frac{\$29,167\,billion}{126/100} = \frac{\$29,167\,billion}{1.26} = \$23,148\,billion.$$

Between 2010 and 2024, the rate of economic growth in real GDP is calculated as follows:

$$Percent\ change = \frac{2024\,real\,GDP - 2010\,real\,GDP}{2010\,real\,GDP} \times 100$$

$$= \frac{\$23,148\,billion - \$16,721\,billion}{\$16,721\,billion} \times 100$$

$$= 0.384 \times 100 = 38.4\%$$

The calculation demonstrates that, between 2010 and 2024, the US economy increased the real production of output by more than 38 percent.

THE COSTS OF INFLATION

As the study of macroeconomics makes clear, two main economic problems exist: inflation and unemployment. When the unemployment rate rises, workers lose their jobs. But why is inflation a problem? Why do policy makers in central banks worry when the inflation rate rises above the target rate of 2 percent? When prices rise, three types of costs exist.

MENU COSTS

When producers alter prices, *menu costs* exist. In modern economies, the prices of the items consumers purchase are listed online, in retail establishments, or on supermarket shelves. This information informs the consumers with respect to their willingness and ability to purchase output. Menu costs exist when firms allocate time and resources to the process of updating the prices of their goods and services. These actions replace other business activities. Specific menu costs include altering websites, changing price tags, and updating menus. When firms minimize menu costs, the output prices become "sticky," not adjusting to changing economic conditions.

SHOE-LEATHER COSTS

Shoe-leather costs refer to the transaction costs from inflation. A relatively high inflation rate discourages individuals from holding money in the form of cash. In this case, the purchasing power of money declines, including the money in bank accounts. Two outcomes occur. First, individuals spend their money on goods and services, before the prices increase further. Second, individuals transfer money from their bank accounts into other assets, such as electronic currency, financial assets, or foreign currency. The shoe-leather costs refer to the extra time and effort to go to the bank to withdraw money. Countries with high inflation rates experience substantial shoe-leather costs.

UNIT-OF-ACCOUNT COSTS

When inflation reduces the reliability of money to serve as a unit of measurement, *unit-of-account costs* exist. One of the characteristics of money is that it serves as a measure of value. The measure of value allows consumers to compare different goods and services. Because markets value the output in terms of money, individuals have the ability to record the value of assets, debts, and transactions. But a relatively high inflation rate degrades the measurement role of money. The reason is that, with inflation, the purchasing power of money declines, reducing the quality of economic decision making. Because of the uncertainty from changes in the unit of account, individuals make decisions in a less efficient way.

INFLATION EXPECTATIONS

In macroeconomics, inflation expectations are important. Why is this the case? Two views exist. First, the traditional view argues that policy makers in the central bank use inflation expectations to predict future inflation rates, informing their economic forecasts. The process of forecasting strengthens monetary policy by providing more information about the future change in the price level. This view holds that inflation expectations benefit individuals who participate in financial markets, buying and selling assets such as stock and bonds. If the individuals view inflation to be a future problem, they purchase more stocks. In inflationary economies, stocks normally have a higher rate of return.

Second, the market view argues that inflation expectations matter because they impact the economic behavior of both firms and households. For firms, inflation expectations impact their prices and wages. If they expect the inflation rate to rise, they will increase prices. At the same time, workers will demand higher wages. For households, inflation expectations impact the decisions to consume and save. If households expect a future increase in the inflation rate, they will buy more goods and services today. This *intertemporal substitution* means that consumers substitute their consumption between different periods. The implication is that, when current consumption increases, saving decreases.

In this context, inflation becomes a self-fulfilling prophecy. An expectation of higher prices causes the inflation rate to rise. If producers and consumers expect higher future prices, they make production and consumption decisions that create this outcome. A psychological effect occurs when households hedge against future inflation by consuming more goods and services today. A wage-price spiral occurs when workers demand higher wages in response to inflation expectations, causing firms to raise prices.

REDISTRIBUTIVE EFFECTS

As this chapter demonstrates, there is a difference between *relative prices* and *average prices*. Relative prices, which are always changing, are the price of one good or service in comparison to the price of another good or service. The price of a shirt may increase without altering the average price level as long as the price of pants or another item decreases. An increase in the relative price of shirts means that they are more expensive in comparison to pants.

In periods of inflation, deflation, or a stable average price level, changes in relative prices occur. With consumers purchasing thousands of goods and services, higher relative prices for products signals to producers to increase their output. But an increase in average prices (inflation) does not create the same outcome. If all prices increase at the same rate, the price changes for specific items do not provide the same market incentives.

The distinction between relative prices and average prices provides a context for the redistributive effects of inflation. Even though inflation makes some people worse off, it makes other people better off. The reason is that people own different things, while selling different goods and services, including labor.

Inflation leads to a redistribution of income and wealth, not an overall decline in either measure. First, the individuals with fixed incomes that do not rise with inflation bear a greater burden. Examples include private pensioners and laborers with multiyear contracts. Second, when inflation occurs, the prices of some goods and services rise more than others. The individuals who consume these items experience a greater burden. Third, when the average price level rises, the real value of savings falls. Holding assets leads to a rate of return, but a higher price level cuts into the gains. Overall, these income effects, price effects, and wealth effects serve as the redistributive mechanisms of inflation, leading to speculation and uncertainty.

KEY TERMS

aggregate price level
average prices
base period
Consumer Price Index
core inflation
cost-push inflation
deflation
demand-pull inflation
inflation
inflation rate
intertemporal substitution
menu costs

Personal Consumption Expenditures Index
price index
Producer Price Index
real interest rate
relative prices
shoe-leather costs
unit-of-account costs

FURTHER READING

Josifidis, Kosta and Supic, Novica. 2023. "Is There a Trade-Off Between Global Inflation and the Great Resignation in the United States?" *Journal of Economic Issues*, 57 (2): 499–506.

Watkins, John. 2023. "Corporate Power and the Return of Inflation." *Journal of Economic Issues*, 57 (2): 507–513.

Weber, Michael, D'Acunto, Francesco, Gorodnichenko, Yuriy and Coibion, Olivier. 2022. "The Subjective Inflation Expectations of Households and Firms: Measurement, Determinants, and Implications." *Journal of Economic Perspectives*, 36 (3): 157–184.

PART II
FOUNDATIONS OF ECONOMIC GROWTH

5

ECONOMIC GROWTH

THE IMPORTANCE OF ECONOMIC GROWTH

Economic growth means an increase in the production of output. The process is important because it transforms poor economies into those with increasing levels of wealth and economic resources. The economies of China, India, and South Korea serve as examples. Through urbanization, industrialization, and economic growth, these countries transformed from less-developed and agrarian societies to industrialized countries. They produce electronics, retail items, vehicles, and many other forms of output for both domestic and foreign markets. The results are noteworthy. The countries have increased their national income.

But for advanced economies, why does economic growth matter? The answer is that it increases the *standard of living* of individuals. The standard of living refers to the level of comfort, income, material goods, and wealth available to a country's residents. A higher standard of living transforms the way people live. With a higher standard of living, more people are able to afford the material comforts of life, including cars, cellphones, and homes. But an increase in the standard of living also leads to better medical care and more nutritious diets. Countries that increase their natural resources and labor force, educate and train workers, and increase their physical capital experience rising living standards.

For countries around the world, the question of interest is whether the standard of living is rising or falling. If it is rising, the country is able to improve the lives of its residents. This trend is important because it correlates with important socio-economic

DOI: 10.4324/9781003678700-7

variables, including health and the quality of life. Higher living standards, for example, are correlated with longer life expectancies. If a country's standard of living is falling, however, the residents do not experience better lives.

Because of these important outcomes, the chapter discusses the standard of living, economic growth in the short run and long run, achieving economic growth, government promotion of economic growth, and intangible capital.

STANDARD OF LIVING

Economists measure the change in the standard of living with the ratio of the growth of real GDP per capita to population growth:

$$Change\ in\ the\ standard\ of\ living = \frac{Growth\ in\ real\ GDP\ per\ capita}{Population\ growth}$$

Three possibilities exist:

- When the growth in real GDP > population growth, the standard of living rises
- When the growth in real GDP < population growth, the standard of living falls
- When the growth in real GDP = population growth, the standard of living remains constant

Of course, the change in real GDP per capita or population could be negative. In this case, the standard of living would adjust. If the real GDP per capita decreases while the population increases, the standard of living declines. Because the ratio determines the change in the standard of living, the variables in the numerator and denominator exist as important indicators.

GROWTH IN REAL GDP PER CAPITA

As Table 5.1 demonstrates, many countries experience a rising level of real GDP per capita over a specific period of time, including China, India, South Korea, and the United States (US).

Table 5.1 Real GDP per capita

Country	2015	2017	2019	2021	2023
China	$8,016	$8,814	$10,143	$12,617	$12,614
India	$1,584	$1,950	$2,041	$2,239	$2,480
South Korea	$37,907	$31,600	$31,902	$35,125	$33,121
United States	$57,040	$60,322	$65,604	$71,318	$82,769

Source: World Bank, https://data.worldbank.org/indicator/NY.GDP.PCAP.CD?locations=US-KR-IN-CN

When the variable increases, the average output per person rises, rather than the price level. But for the countries in the table the difference in the size of real GDP per capita is high. Compared to India, the output per person in the US is many times larger.

To calculate the change in the standard of living, the numerator in the above equation uses annual growth rates in real GDP per capita (Table 5.2). During 2015–2023, the countries experienced a positive level of real GDP per capita in most of the years. In 2020, the first year of the coronavirus pandemic, real GDP per capita was negative in three of the four countries.

During 2015–2023, the average annual growth rate differs by country:

- China: 5.5%
- India: 4.8%
- South Korea: 2.2%
- United States: 1.9%

Table 5.2 Annual growth rates in real GDP per capita (%)

Country	2015	2016	2017	2018	2019	2020	2021	2022	2023
China	6.4	6.2	6.3	6.3	5.6	2.0	8.4	3.0	5.4
India	6.7	7.0	5.6	5.3	2.8	-6.7	8.8	6.1	7.2
South Korea	2.3	2.5	2.9	2.5	1.9	-0.8	4.4	2.8	1.3
United States	2.2	1.1	1.8	2.4	2.1	-3.1	5.9	2.1	2.4

Source: World Bank, https://data.worldbank.org/indicator/NY.GDP.PCAP.KD.ZG?locations=KR-CN-IN-US

Due to the financial power of compounding, small but consistent growth rates lead to large changes. To approximate the number of years it takes for a variable to double, the Rule of 70 applies:

$$Number\ of\ years\ to\ double\ = \frac{70}{growth\ rate\ (\%)}$$

The difference between the average annual growth rates leads to a significant difference in the number of years it takes for real GDP per capita to double:

$$Number\ of\ years\ to\ double_{China}\ = \frac{70}{5.5}\ =\ 12.7\ years$$

$$Number\ of\ years\ to\ double_{India}\ = \frac{70}{4.8}\ =\ 14.6\ years$$

$$Number\ of\ years\ to\ double_{South\ Korea}\ = \frac{70}{2.2}\ =\ 31.8\ years$$

$$Number\ of\ years\ to\ double_{United\ States}\ = \frac{70}{1.9}\ =\ 36.8\ years$$

Given the average growth rates, China's real GDP per capita doubles in 12.7 years. But it takes 36.8 years for real GDP per capita to double in the US.

Although the Rule of 70 does not provide an exact forecast for compounding, its straightforward application provides a useful tool. When the economy grows at a faster rate than the population, the increase in output leads to a rise in living standards. But economic growth does not eliminate poverty. The inequalities of opportunity and wealth prevent the benefits of economic growth from flowing to all households, especially those in the lowest income quintile

In general, if real GDP per capita is rising, more goods and services are available. Consumers are in a stronger position to purchase them. But real GDP per capita does not include several important opportunities, including changes in the quality of goods and services, changes in the quality of life, and the value of unpaid work. For the households in the lowest income quintile, these factors exist as important aspects of their daily lives. Therefore, while real GDP per capita is a useful statistic, it is difficult to quantify factors such as the quality of life. The rising living standards for the majority of the population may exclude the households with fewer economic opportunities.

POPULATION GROWTH

Population growth impacts economic conditions, including the change in the production of output, generation of income, and distribution of outcomes. The projection is for the world population to peak at 10.5 billion people at the end of the century. But this chapter demonstrates that the important variable to consider is the population growth rate for individual countries. If the population growth rate exceeds the growth in real GDP per capita, a country's living standards decline. What are the components of the population growth rate? What are the trends for countries around the world? The components of the population growth rate are the birth rate, death rate, and rate of migration. Early in the process of economic development, both birth rates and death rates are high, leading to a relatively stable population growth rate. But when income rises, healthcare and working conditions improve. The death rate falls at a faster rate than the birth rate, leading to population growth. A positive level of migration into the country accelerates the process.

When the country reaches high-income status, the members of society access education and healthcare. The birth rate falls, the death rate persists at a low level, and the population growth rate stabilizes. Eventually, developed countries may experience declining population growth rates: birth rates fall below the replacement level of two births for every couple. Many developed countries experience this outcome, including Germany, Italy, Japan, Russia, and South Korea.

As long as real GDP per capita rises, a declining population growth rate contributes to a rising standard of living. But eventually a lower population leads to an aging society, a decrease in demand, economic stagnation, a smaller workforce, and a strain on social services. The economy struggles to maintain its production, leading to a decrease in real GDP per capita.

RISING LIVING STANDARDS

If a country generates a higher level of income while implementing appropriate social policies, its residents benefit from a rising standard of living. The reason is that a higher standard of living leads to several positive outcomes, including greater purchasing power, a higher level of educational achievement, a lower level of poverty, a higher material existence, and social security. The difference in life expectancy between high-income and low-income countries is vast, ranging from around 80 years for the former to around 60 years for the latter.

ECONOMIC GROWTH IN THE SHORT RUN AND LONG RUN

Economic growth leads to a higher level of output. By using real GDP per capita as a measurement of economic growth, economists assess whether economies experience rising living standards. But a difference exists between economic growth in the short run and the long run.

ECONOMIC GROWTH IN THE SHORT RUN

In the short run, the economy's productive capacity is fixed. Firms have a specific amount of factory space. In this time frame, the economy produces a certain amount of goods and services with its economic resources and technology. Without additional investments in physical capital and other productive resources, the economy's potential output remains constant. In the short run, economic growth occurs when the economy uses existing but underutilized resources. Firms employ workers without jobs, use empty factory space, and fill abandoned space in shopping centers with new stores. When obstacles are eliminated that prevent the economy from using economic resources to their fullest extent (such as restrictions on the use of land), or the economy is recovering from recession, short-run growth occurs. Using the production possibility curve, short-run economic growth means a movement from inside the curve to the frontier (Figure 5.1).

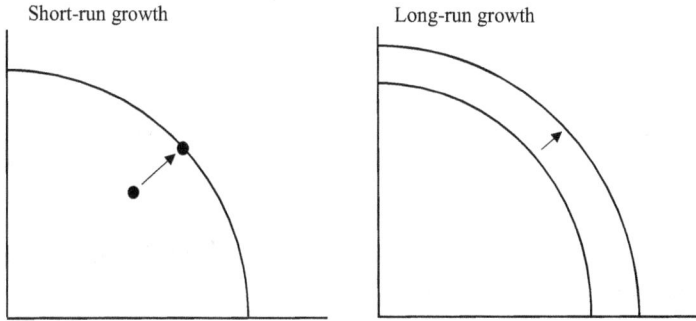

Figure 5.1 Economic growth in the short run and long run

ECONOMIC GROWTH IN THE LONG RUN

In the long run, the economy expands its productive capacity and achieves economic growth by increasing its economic resources or using existing resources more productively. When economic growth occurs in the long run, the production possibility curve shifts out (Figure 5.1). Examples include a higher level of human capital for the workforce, technological advances that make better use of economic resources, or the availability of more natural resources. The use of artificial intelligence, for example, enhances economic productivity by increasing labor efficiency, the quality of service, and the ability to synthesize information. When the productive capacity of the economy rises, the economy has the ability to produce more output.

SOURCES OF ECONOMIC GROWTH

To achieve economic growth, the economy has to produce more output. In some economies, economic growth occurs because the labor force grows at a faster rate than the population. A generation of people starts working. A high employment rate leads to an increase in real GDP per capita. This outcome means a larger number of people are working compared to the labor force. But the employment rate does not always rise. At the limit, all eligible people are in the labor force and firms are not able to employ additional workers. When the employment rate decreases, it becomes more difficult for the economy to achieve an increase in real GDP per capita.

PRODUCTIVITY

In the above example, to offset the decrease in the employment rate, the economy must increase the amount of output per worker, the measure of *productivity*. In this context, an increase in productivity serves as an important factor for economic growth. The idea is that the economy is able to produce more output with the same economic resources. The most common measure is *labor productivity*, a ratio of the economy's total output to the number of hours worked:

$$Labor\, productivity = \frac{Total\, output}{Total\, employment}$$

In the US, real GDP was equal to \$22.96 trillion in 2023, according to the Bureau of Economic Analysis. In 2024, real GDP was equal to \$23.53 trillion. Between 2023 and 2024, the economy's level of employment increased from 161.12 million to 161.66 million. For the two years, labor productivity is:

$$Labor\, productivity_{2023} = \frac{Total\, output}{Total\, employment} = \frac{\$22.96\, trillion}{161.12\, million} = \$142,502$$

$$Labor\, productivity_{2024} = \frac{Total\, output}{Total\, employment} = \frac{\$23.53\, trillion}{161.66\, million} = \$145,552$$

Compared to most of the countries in the world, this is a large amount of output per worker. For all economies, the rise in productivity leads to economic growth.

FACTORS OF PRODUCTION

To achieve economic growth, an economy must acquire additional resources or produce output in a more productive manner. The economic resources, introduced in Chapter 1, are categorized as four factors of production. First, land and natural resources (N) entail the areas where production occurs and the resources that come from land, such as minerals, natural gas, oil, and water.

Second, labor (L) includes the efforts of individuals to contribute to the process of production. Related to labor, human capital (H) refers to the education and training that improves worker performance. Third, physical capital (K) includes the human-made resources that contribute to the production of output, including computers, equipment, machines, and tools. Fourth, entrepreneurial ability describes the drive, skills, and vision necessary to create new production processes and products, and the management of the risk of bringing new forms of innovation to the economy. In the process of production, this factor is the technology (T) that increases the productivity of the economic resources. By identifying economic opportunities, entrepreneurs create value for the land, labor, human capital, and physical capital.

PRODUCTION FUNCTION

The *production function* describes the maximum amount of output from different combinations of economic resources and technology. Although many production functions exist, most demonstrate that the production of output equals technology times the factors of production:

$$Output = T \times f(N, L, H, K)$$

The latter part of the equation means that the production of output is a function of economic resource inputs. For example, technology companies emphasize human capital (highly skilled labor) and physical capital (computers and servers). Manufacturing companies emphasize the land where factories exist, laborers, and physical capital such as equipment and machines. Every firm uses a unique combination of economic resources. In the long run, more economic resources lead to a higher level of output, shifting the production possibility curve outward.

The question is how economic growth impacts the average person. To answer the question, economists alter the production function to measure output per person. Suppose an increase in the amount of economic resources leads to an equivalent increase in output. Dividing all economic resources by L provides the production function in terms of output per worker:

$$Output\,per\,wor\,ker = T \times f\left(\frac{N}{L}, \frac{L}{L}, \frac{H}{L}, \frac{K}{L}\right)$$

In the equation, the output per worker equals technology times a function of land and natural resources per worker, human capital per worker, and physical capital per worker. Because the equation focuses on output per worker, having more laborers does not necessarily translate into economic growth: $L/L = 1$. But an increase in the other variables leads to economic growth.

REASONS FOR ECONOMIC GROWTH

The production function demonstrates how economic resources are converted into output. The level of productivity refers to the extent to which economic resources contribute to a given level of output. When productivity rises, two outcomes occur. First, a given level of economic resources produce more output. Second, fewer economic resources produce the same level of output.

In this context, productivity is linked to wages. As a worker's productivity rises, wages rise. Firms offer higher compensation to the workers that contribute more to the production process. For many developed countries, this serves as a reason that the living standards are higher.

For economic growth to occur, the factors of production play an important role. More economic resources lead to an increase in the production of output. In addition, a higher level of technology means that economic resources are more productive, leading to economic growth. Highly productive economies produce output of greater value, leading to a higher level of real GDP per capita. Because the labor force works with human capital, physical capital, and technology, the economies that adjust to changing market conditions produce a variety of goods and services and high-priced products. But what factors increase productivity and economic growth? To answer the question, the production function provides a framework for analysis.

More land and natural resources contribute to the production of output. But they do not serve as major factors of economic growth. When economies tap into abundant sources of land and natural resources, they benefit from these contributions, but only if the economies use the economic resources productively. Countries that experience abundance in this area, such as Canada with timber and Saudi Arabia with oil, have the potential to experience higher growth rates if they use the resources efficiently.

Population growth leads to an increase in the supply of labor. For countries that experience fertility at or below the replacement rate, population growth is due to immigration. In addition, an increase in the labor force participation rate leads to a greater number of workers. In many countries, as more women enter the labor force, the participation rate rises. An increase in the labor force leads to a higher level of output, but not a higher level of output per worker. For this factor to increase real GDP per capita, an increase in the quality of the labor force must occur.

An increase in the quality of the labor force occurs when workers produce more goods and services. An increase in human capital leads to this outcome. A better educated and trained workforce possesses more knowledge and skills. Societies increase human capital through education, on-the-job training, and an improvement in the skill sets of workers. With investments in human capital, the quality of the labor force improves.

A higher level of physical capital per worker serves as a major contributor to economic growth. When individuals have more computers, equipment, and machines, their productivity levels rise. In many industries, including electronics, telecommunications, and vehicles, a higher capital-to-labor ratio increases output per worker and income. This is an important reason why the US, South Korea, Japan, and Germany have experienced a rise in living standards. Many developing countries, in contrast, have large populations, but lack the physical capital necessary to experience an increase in productivity.

Diminishing returns accompany physical capital. Economies employ the most essential forms of physical capital first. Additional units of physical capital increase the production of output, but each additional unit contributes less. As a result, countries with abundant physical capital do not experience the same gains on the next unit as countries with little physical capital.

This is the reason that developing countries with lower GDP per capita may initially experience higher growth rates, a concept known as the *catch-up effect*. With the use of physical capital, these countries benefit from higher returns. China serves as an example with the development of high-speed rail, the utilization of advanced production techniques, and the equipment and machines that facilitate assembly-line processes. China adopts the technology of advanced economies. But the catch-up effect does not apply on a universal basis. Other factors play a role, including the effective forms of governance and efficient markets, which are not present in all developing countries.

In summary, the factors that increase productivity and lead to economic growth are:

- An increase in the amount of land and natural resources per capita
- An increase in the quality of the labor force
- An increase in the level of physical capital per capita

TOTAL FACTOR PRODUCTIVITY

How efficiently an economy uses its economic resources determines the level of productivity. Economies that have more natural resources, human capital, and physical capital produce more goods and services. But *total factor productivity* (TFP)—the factors that influence the effectiveness of economic resources—contributes to the process. In the production function, TFP represents the residual attributable to technological progress (T). First, TFP results from innovation, including the creation of continuous feedback loops, cross-functional collaboration, and employee recognition platforms. Second, TFP results from an improvement in the efficiency of economic resources. The examples include adaptation to changing economic conditions, more effective time management, and streamlining economic processes. Third, TFP results from a change in the scale of economic activity. The examples include the achievement of economies of scale, lower average total costs, and efficiency gains. Together, the innovation, efficiency gains, and economies of scale increase the effectiveness of economic resources.

GOVERNMENT PROMOTION OF ECONOMIC GROWTH

Government spending contributes to the process of economic growth. Public sector interventions take different forms, impacting TFP.

First, by overseeing the financial and legal systems, the government facilitates economic growth. These systems promote business contracts, financial transactions, property rights, and resource allocation. The enforcement of business contracts ensures production and purchasing commitments. An effective financial system facilitates borrowing and lending and promotes a stable currency. The protection of property rights facilitates economic exchange and incentivizes productive activities. The promotion of resource allocation maximizes efficiency and productivity, leading to the best use of economic resources. In summary, with effective financial and legal systems, the government fosters:

- Business contracts
- Financial transactions
- Property rights
- Resource allocation

Second, the government promotes productive markets. This focus contributes to both consumption and production. The correct mix of policies and regulations provides the incentive for economic activity, while creating an environment conducive for work. The latter means that individuals have benefits, fair compensation, and a safe working environment. The promotion of economic freedom means that suppliers produce the output that maximizes profit. Individuals are free to choose what to consume. But the government must address the problem of market failure, when markets lead to an inefficient distribution of goods and services. In summary, the promotion of productive markets advances:

- Economic activity
- Economic freedom

Third, the government purchases goods and services. An important area of spending is human capital when the government allocates resources for public education and financial aid. Another area of spending is physical capital, the country's *infrastructure*. This area consists of the systems that support the country's economy, energy, environment, and transportation. For example, the energy system consists of the power-generating plants and the power lines. The transportation network includes roads and rail lines. These tangible forms of output strengthen the economy's productive capacity. The government spends money on technological advances, funding research centers and individual projects. In summary, with direct purchases, the government promotes:

- Human capital
- Physical capital
- Technology

INTANGIBLE CAPITAL

As this chapter explains, the standard of living of a country's residents depends on the rate of growth of real GDP per capita relative to population growth. The former variable, in turn, depends on the production of output. The production function demonstrates that, as firms employ more economic resources and technology, the production of output increases. But the production function does not explain the entirety of the process. The *intangible capital* fills the gap. It is knowledge-based and productive capital, but lacks a physical presence.

Three categories exist. Digitized information includes databases and software. Innovative property includes expenditures on the creation of new products, exploration, industrial design, and research and development. Economic competencies include branding, distributional networks, market research, supply chains, and training. These forms of intangible capital contribute to the productivity of firms and economic growth of the economy.

With intangible capital, two fundamental properties exist. First, the creation of intangible capital means forgoing current investment to achieve more future output. Second, because intangible capital consists of information without a physical form, it requires a *storage medium*, such as a computer (for a customer list or software program), electronic file (for a copyright, design, or patent), or individual (for an idea or innovation). Firms use algorithms to store computer code and software. Drawings contain logos. Teams of workers store managerial processes and operational procedures.

Because firms employ intangible capital in multiple places, the firms apply it simultaneously in production. Multiple employees apply company innovations and use the outcomes of new designs. With intangible capital, firms reap the benefits of economies of scale.

KEY TERMS

catch-up effect
infrastructure
intangible capital
labor productivity
production function
productivity
standard of living
storage medium
total factor productivity

FURTHER READING

Corrado, Carol, Haskel, Jonathan, Jona-Lasinio, Cecilia and Iommi, Massimiliano. 2022. "Intangible Capital and Modern Economies." *Journal of Economic Perspectives*, 36 (3): 3–28.

Crouzet, Nicolas, Eberly, Janice, Eisfeldt, Andrea and Papanikolaou, Dimitris. 2022. "The Economics of Intangible Capital." *Journal of Economic Perspectives*, 36 (3): 29–52.

Feldstein, Martin. 2017. "Underestimating the Real Growth of GDP, Personal Income, and Productivity." *Journal of Economic Perspectives*, 31 (2): 145–164.

6

SAVINGS, INVESTMENT, AND THE FINANCIAL SYSTEM

NEW BUSINESS ACTIVITY

When firms begin, they allocate money for startup costs. Businesses in different industries spend money on equipment, insurance, inventory, legal and accounting fees, and worker salaries. Specific examples include the computers and laptops for office workers, the rent for operating space, and software programs for data analytics. In the early stages, the firms create budgets, estimate fixed and variable costs, forecast demand, manage the flow of cash, and track expenditures. All of these economic activities require money. But the entrepreneurs that start the businesses may not have the financing. What are the ways to secure funding? One way is to secure funding from a financial investor in exchange for shares of ownership or future earnings. But this option dilutes the value of the business, because the investor establishes future claims. Another option is to obtain funding from the *financial system*. This is the system of institutions and markets that channels money from savers to investors.

Savings and investment serve as key components of economic growth. In the long run, savings and investment facilitate higher levels of production. When economic agents save a larger percentage of GDP, the economy has more resources available for investment. The investment enhances the economy's productive capacity, facilitating innovation and a higher level of production. The investments in equipment and machines for firms and education and training for workers increase productivity and the quantity of output per worker. The process leads to job creation and economic resilience. The overall result is an increase in the standard of living.

DOI: 10.4324/9781003678700-8

This chapter explains how the economy coordinates savings and investment, and how this coordination contributes to economic growth. In the economy, some economic agents want to save a portion of their current income for future opportunities. Other economic agents want to borrow money to finance investments in new and growing businesses. What mechanism coordinates these actions? What ensures that the demand for funds by borrowers is satisfied by the supply of funds by lenders? The answer is the financial system. It channels saving into investment, oversees financial markets, and serves as an important institution for economic growth. To analyze these topics, the chapter discusses savings and investment, the financial system, the saving decision, the investment decision, and the market for loanable funds.

SAVINGS AND INVESTMENT

The economic activity that occurs in the financial system is important for the overall economy. The institutions, including banks and financial markets, coordinate savings and investment. But to understand the importance of savings and investment for economic growth, it is useful to consider these concepts as macroeconomic variables in national income accounts. The national income accounts include important identities, which are equations that are true because of the way they are formulated. Identities clarify how variables relate to one another. Recall the GDP (Y) identity, which shows that Y equals the summation of consumption (C), investment (I), government expenditure (G), and net exports ($X - M$):

$$Y = C + I + G + (X - M)$$

The reason that the equation is an identity is that the expenditure that exists with GDP on the left side corresponds to one of the four components on the right side. The definition and measurement of the variables mean that the identity always holds.

To begin, assume a closed economy without a foreign sector. The assumption provides a context for savings and investment. A simplification of the GDP identity yields:

$$Y = C + I + G$$

In the new identity, GDP exists as the sum of consumption, investment, and government expenditure. Every unit of production is consumed by households, invested by businesses, or purchased by the government.

To continue, investment is isolated:

$$Y - C - G = I$$

The left side represents the economy's remaining income after paying for consumption and government spending. This total equals savings, denoted as S. Because $S = Y - C - G$, it follows that saving equals investment:

$$S = I$$

To understand the concept of national savings, suppose that T equals the taxes the government collects from economic agents minus the transfer payments to households. The model formulates national savings in two ways:

$$S = Y - C - G$$

or

$$S = (Y - T - C) + (T - G)$$

The two identities are the same, except the second identity includes T in two places. Because T is subtracted and added, the two variables cancel each other. In the second identity, the right side includes *private savings* $(Y - T - C)$ and *public savings* $(T - G)$. The former is the amount of money that remains for households after they pay taxes and consume output. The latter is the amount of money the government has after its purchases, revealing two possibilities:

$$When\, T - G > 0,\, a\, budget\, surplus\, exists$$

$$When\, T - G < 0,\, a\, budget\, deficit\, exists$$

The accumulation of annual deficits leads to government debt. The public debt is the amount of money a government owes to its creditors, accumulated over time, to both domestic and foreign lenders. Public borrowing is necessary to finance spending that exceeds government tax revenue.

Because $S = I$, savings must equal investment for the economy as a whole. But why? What process channels the flow of savings to the process of investment, the latter meaning the purchase of new capital such as buildings or equipment? The answer is the financial system, which provides the markets and intermediaries that facilitate financial exchange.

THE FINANCIAL SYSTEM

For the economy as a whole, the financial system channels money from savers to borrowers. On one side of the market, the economic agents who save spend less than they earn. They use the savings for different reasons, such as putting children through college, planning for retirement, or exercising the precautionary demand for money. Savers supply money to the financial system with the expectation that they will receive it back in the future plus interest. On the other side of the market, households borrow funds to facilitate the purchase of a home, car, or another item. Firms borrow money for capital investment. For borrowers, the expectation is that they will repay the money in the future plus interest. In the context of direct finance (through financial markets) and indirect finance (through financial intermediaries), the financial system facilitates this exchange (Figure 6.1).

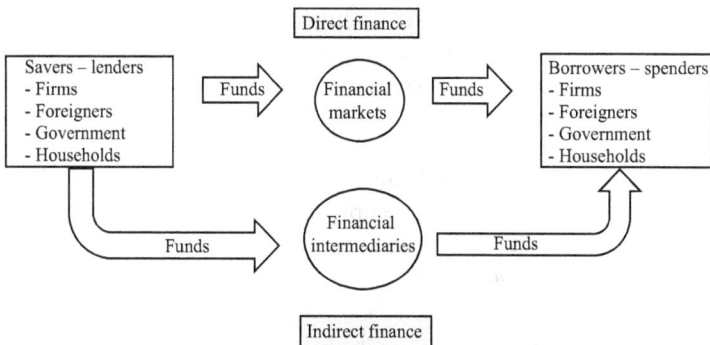

Figure 6.1 The financial system

FINANCIAL MARKETS

In the process of direct finance, *financial markets* channel funds from savers to borrowers. Those who save have a surplus of funds, so they lend. Those who spend have a shortage of funds, so they borrow. In financial markets, firms, foreign economic agents, the government, and households serve as both savers and borrowers. In the process of direct finance, the spenders borrow directly from lenders by purchasing *securities*, which are tradable financial instruments. For the economic agents that buy securities, they are assets. But for the economic agents that issue securities, they are liabilities. For example, a company may issue *stocks*, which are shares of ownership, in order to raise money. In addition, a firm may need to borrow money to pay for new machinery and equipment, so it issues *bonds*, which are debt securities that require payments for a period of time.

For the economy as a whole, why are financial markets important? The economic agents who save are not the same as the ones who borrow. Financial markets channel money from the economic agents who lack productive investment opportunities to the economic agents who have the opportunities. Several important outcomes occur. First, financial markets lead to an efficient allocation of money. This outcome contributes to a higher level of production. Second, financial markets enhance the well-being of individuals by improving the timing of their purchases. Through the process of borrowing, the individuals may buy a house or vehicle without the possession of the entire sum of money. Finally, financial markets provide *liquidity*, meaning the ease with which economic agents convert assets into cash without a decrease in value. Holding liquid assets enhances the ability of firms or households to meet short-term obligations.

A firm may obtain funds in two ways. One method is to issue *equities*, such as stocks, which are claims to the net income of a firm. An example of long-term securities because they do not have maturity dates, equities often make periodic payments to their holders in the form of *dividends*. Owning stock means an economic agent owns a part of the firm. Another method is to issue *debt instruments*, such as bonds, which require holders to make regular payments of principal and interest until a maturity date. A short-term debt instrument has a maturity date of less than one year; an intermediate-term instrument has a maturity date of between one and ten years; a long-term security has a maturity date of more than ten years.

A difference exists between the types of financial markets. The *primary market* includes new securities, such as stocks or bonds, issued by firms or government, and the purchase of the securities by economic agents. This market provides money for the entities who need it, which fuels investment, innovation, and economic growth. The *secondary market* consists of securities that have already been bought and sold. This market establishes the true market value of securities, provides a method for economic agents to invest, and injects liquidity into the economy. Together, the primary and secondary markets provide borrowers with the opportunity to raise money and lenders the opportunity to generate a rate of return.

An additional way to distinguish between financial markets is the length of maturity of the securities. The *money market* is where short-term debt instruments of less than one year are bought and sold. For the economy, the money market allocates money according to demand, distributes liquid assets among economic agents, and hedges against short-term risk. The *capital market* is where debt instruments with maturities longer than one year and equities are bought and sold. For the economy, the capital market diversifies investment opportunities, promotes innovation, and supports economic growth. Because the financial instruments in the money market are more widely traded, they are more liquid than the financial instruments in the capital market.

FINANCIAL INTERMEDIARIES

With indirect finance, economic agents borrow funds from lenders through *financial intermediaries*, such as banks and credit unions. Financial intermediaries facilitate the flow of money from savers to investors. The process occurs when the intermediaries borrow funds from the savers-lenders and loan the money to the borrowers-spenders. A bank or credit union raises money by providing checking and savings accounts to the public. It then uses the funds to make loans to firms or individuals, or purchase bonds in the open market. The overall impact is to transfer money from the savers-lenders to the borrowers-spenders, facilitating economic activity. The process of financial intermediation serves as the primary route for the movement of money in the economy. The process is important for economic growth, but it generates costs.

First, information costs exist with financial transactions. Economic agents incur costs by searching for financial information. The problem is that the borrowers may not have the same information as the lenders. This inequality is called *asymmetric information*. For example, a bank normally has more information about the risk of a loan than a borrower. The problem of asymmetric information exists in two contexts: before the transaction and after the transaction. Before the transaction, the presence of *adverse selection* means that a specific category of borrowers is likely to seek loans but may create adverse outcomes because of bad credit scores. After the transaction, the presence of *moral hazard* consists of the risk that the borrowers may undertake undesirable behavior and experience an inability to pay back the loans. Because adverse selection and moral hazard impede the efficient flow of money, financial intermediaries screen borrowers and establish terms of engagement.

Second, when savers-lenders provide funds, they assume the *risk* of financial investment. The risk refers to the uncertainty of the future rate of return. When economic agents purchase stocks in the capital market, they assume market risk. The market may set a higher or lower value for the stock. But through the process of risk sharing, financial intermediaries reduce the exposure to risk. They accomplish this objective by selling assets with identifiable risk characteristics, such as a specific rate of return and length of time to maturity. The decrease in transaction cost leads to *asset transformation*, when riskier assets are transformed into safer assets. As a practical measure, financial intermediaries recommend the diversification of financial portfolios, which leads to a reduction in risk.

Third, a transaction cost occurs when economic agents allocate time and money for financial transactions. Financial intermediaries decrease the transaction cost with their expertise and ability to take advantage of economies of scale. The provision of more financial opportunities lowers the cost of additional transactions. For example, the provision by banks of free checking accounts simplifies the process of paying bills. In addition, banks offer free ATM services, bank transfers, and credit card usage. These processes decrease cost, increase efficiency, and raise the level of accessibility to the financial system.

THE DECISION TO SAVE

The decision to save money means the deferral of current consumption in order to increase future consumption. For households, the rate of saving out of current income exists as an important element of financial security. For the economy, the rate of saving is correlated with economic growth. When the population is growing, more people are in the labor force, relative to the number of retirees. In this context, the overall level of savings increases: more workers are saving, compared to the number of retirees who are dissaving. The higher the level of population growth, the higher will be the rate of saving, all else equal. Several reasons exist for the decision to save: to accumulate wealth, to allocate money for retirement, to purchase financial investments, to put aside a portion of current income during the working phase of the life cycle, and to satisfy precautionary demand (Table 6.1).

THE DECISION TO INVEST

The reason that firms invest in physical capital such as buildings, equipment, and machines is to make money. The expenditure on investment opportunities is undertaken with the expectation of profit. In two ways, the investment in physical capital links to profitability. First, the investment in physical capital improves the

Table 6.1 Reasons for saving by households

Reason	Explanation
Accumulate wealth	By providing funds for financial, monetary, and real assets, the process of saving facilitates the accumulation of wealth.
Allocate money for retirement	By providing funds for retirement, individuals secure a more stable and prosperous future.
Purchase financial investments	By allocating money for savings, households may purchase financial investments, including stocks, bonds, and mutual funds.
Put aside a portion of current income	By putting aside a portion of current income, economic agents increase their future economic opportunities.
Satisfy precautionary demand	By saving money, households have the ability to establish a buffer against unforeseen circumstances.

profitability of the firm's operations. The firm forecasts an increase in profits if it engages in research and development, expands its productive capacity, implements a new production technique, introduces a new product, or promotes sales. In these cases, added capacity, modernized operating systems, or new equipment position the firm to profit from favorable market conditions. Second, an investment in physical capital reduces the cost of production. Capital equipment increases productivity by supplementing labor.

These are the reasons that the investment in physical capital links to the profitability of firms. But what is the nature of the investment decision? What factors influence the decision to invest in physical capital? The theory of investment provides the answers.

Because entrepreneurs invest in physical capital in the expectation that it will increase profits, new equipment and machinery represent an element of productive returns. Over the life of the physical capital, its value depends on the stream of net income that it generates. In the process, the entrepreneur converts money on hand or borrowed money into capital goods that generate a flow of cash. Over time, the cash flow exists as an expected stream of money because physical capital is durable and continues to yield value. But the size of the expected income stream depends on the material cost and wages that accompany physical capital, the price of the output that flows from the use of physical capital, and the productivity of the physical capital.

To the extent that the firm minimizes cost, the price of output is determined in the market, and the productivity is maximized, the physical capital boosts the firm's profitability. But will the investment generate profit? The process is profitable if the investment yields a stream of money that exceeds the cost of acquiring the physical capital.

In the context of forecasting, the firm is able to estimate the cost, which is the supply price of capital. This is the price that induces the manufacturer of physical capital to produce an additional unit. It is also the price that provides the incentive for the firm to purchase an additional unit. But no matter the durability or the nature of the physical capital, firms must acquire money for the purchase price by using their retained earnings, selling shares of stock, or borrowing money with debt instruments. With these options, the interest rate serves as the cost to the firm of borrowing money to purchase additional physical capital.

Because the firm does not possess full knowledge of the market conditions that determine the stream of income, the estimation of whether the decision will generate a profit is uncertain. When contemplating an increase in productive capacity, a firm may estimate that it is cheaper to buy the assets or merge with another firm. Therefore, the investment by firms is less stable than the consumption by households.

THE MARKET FOR LOANABLE FUNDS

The loanable funds model describes the market for savings and investment. This chapter demonstrates that saving occurs in the presence of excess funds. When economic agents save, they provide money to the loanable funds market. The process occurs directly when an individual buys a bond from a firm, or indirectly when an individual deposits money in a bank. Many reasons exist, including the accumulation of wealth, allocation of money for retirement, accumulation of financial investments, allocation of a portion of income for the future, and satisfaction of precautionary demand. The reward for saving is the interest rate. The additional income from the interest boosts future consumption.

In the market, saving provides the *supply of loanable funds* (S_0), which increases as the interest rate increases (Figure 6.2). As the reward for saving increases, economic agents save more out of current income. As a result, the supply curve slopes upward.

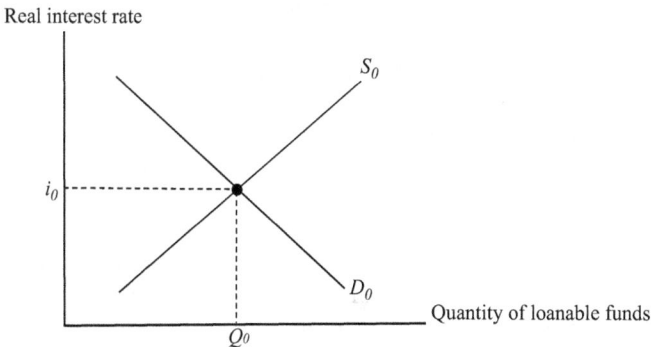

Figure 6.2 Loanable funds market

The *demand for loanable funds* (D_0) comes from the economic agents who need money. The economic agents include firms investing in physical capital, foreign economic agents purchasing currency, governments financing deficits, and households making economic decisions. When a firm borrows money to purchase additional equipment, it demands loanable funds. Other examples include a family securing a mortgage to buy a home, an individual borrowing money to pay for college, or a business expanding its warehouse facilities. The demand curve slopes downward: when interest rates are low, more projects will have a price that is low enough to justify the investment. An economic agent will choose a project if the expected return (benefit) exceeds the price of borrowing (cost). As the interest rate decreases, more projects become profitable. In general, investment is the source of demand in the market.

The real interest rate, which is adjusted for inflation, serves as both the price of borrowing and the reward for saving. It is the amount that economic agents have to pay to borrow money. It is also the amount that economic agents receive when they lend money. A low interest rate reduces the cost of borrowing. But as the interest rate falls, the reward for saving decreases.

EQUILIBRIUM IN THE MARKET FOR LOANABLE FUNDS

The intersection of supply and demand determines the equilibrium interest rate (i_0). At a specific moment, i_0 is the market rate for both borrowing and saving. If a market disequilibrium exists, an adjustment occurs. For example, with the prevailing supply and demand conditions, if the market rate exceeds i_0, the suppliers would save more money, but borrowers would demand less money. The real interest rate would fall. In contrast, if the market rate is less than i_0, the suppliers would save less, but the borrowers would demand more. The real interest rate would rise. In these cases, the real interest rate gravitates to equilibrium, similar to a competitive market for output or economic resources. The loanable funds market is subject to shifts in supply and demand, which alter the equilibrium price and quantity.

SHIFT IN THE SUPPLY OF LOANABLE FUNDS

When a factor alters the willingness of economic agents to save at any real interest rate, the supply curve shifts to the right (increases) or to the left (decreases). Several economic conditions impact the decision, including changes in asset prices, economic forecasts, government deficits, and the incentive to save:

- Asset prices: when income rises, economic agents save more. But when asset prices rise, such as the value of homes or stocks, economic agents feel wealthier and save less. When the savings rate decreases, the supply of loanable funds curve shifts to the left, increasing the real interest rate from i_0 to i_1 and decreasing the quantity of loanable funds from Q_0 to Q_1 (Figure 6.3).
- Economic forecasts: when an economic downturn occurs, individuals forecast an increase in the unemployment rate. The result is an increase in the savings rate. When the level of savings increases, the supply of loanable funds curve shifts to the right, decreasing the real interest rate and increasing the quantity of loanable funds.
- Government deficits: the supply of loanable funds includes the private saving by firms and households and the public saving by the government. If the government experiences a budget surplus, the spending is less than tax revenue. Additional funds

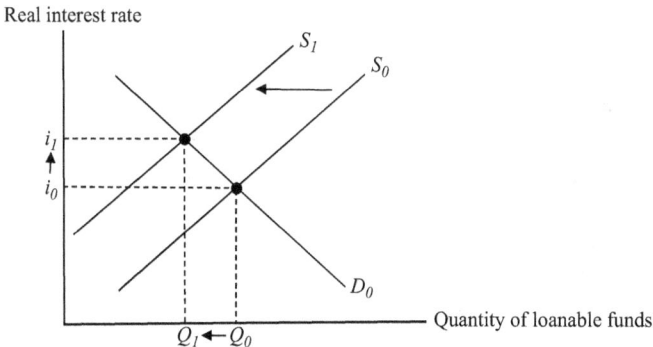

Figure 6.3 Decrease in the supply of loanable funds

flow into the market, and the supply of loanable funds increases. But when the government experiences a budget deficit, the spending exceeds tax revenue. For borrowers and investors, the supply of loanable funds decreases.

- Incentive to save: both firms and the government offer incentives to individuals to alter the savings rate, including retirement plans and tax incentives. When the policies boost savings, the supply of loanable funds curve increases.

SHIFT IN THE DEMAND FOR LOANABLE FUNDS

The factors that cause the demand for loanable funds to shift include changes in business expectations, product demand, regulations, tax incentives, and technological advancements:

- Business expectations: during the expansionary phase of the business cycle, sales expectations rise. When business sentiment increases, the investment demand increases, shifting the demand for loanable funds to the right. The result is an increase in both the real interest rate and quantity of loanable funds in the market.
- Product demand: when the demand for products increases, the return on investment rises. The demand for loanable funds increases, shifting to the right.
- Regulations: regulations by the government alter business investment. When regulations complicate the building process or increase operating costs, the demand for investment falls. In this case, the demand for loanable funds curve shifts to the left, decreasing both the real interest rate and quantity of loanable funds in the market.
- Tax incentives: a policy of investment tax credits by the government decreases the tax payments by firms. These policies boost after-tax returns, increasing investment and the demand for loanable funds.
- Technological advancements: new technologies increase productivity or lead to the creation of new products. These outcomes create the incentive for more production and investment, increasing the demand for loanable funds.

Table 6.2 Shifts in supply and demand

Shift	Change in the real interest rate	Change in the quantity of loanable funds
Supply increases (shifts rightward)	Decrease	Increase
Supply decreases (shifts leftward)	Increase	Decrease
Demand increases (shifts rightward)	Increase	Increase
Demand decreases (shifts leftward)	Decrease	Decrease

CHANGE IN EQUILIBRIUM

In the market, a shift in the supply of loanable funds or demand for loanable funds leads to a new equilibrium. Table 6.2 summarizes the outcomes. Readers are encouraged to draw each graph.

KEY TERMS

adverse selection
asset transformation
asymmetric information
bonds
capital market
debt instruments
demand for loanable funds
dividends
equities
financial intermediaries
financial markets
financial system
liquidity
money market
moral hazard
primary market
private savings
public savings
risk
secondary market
securities
stocks
supply of loanable funds

FURTHER READING

Beshears, John, Choi, James, Laibson, David, Madrian, Brigitte and Milkman, Katherine. 2015. "The Effect of Providing Peer Information on Retirement Savings Decisions." *The Journal of Finance*, 70 (3): 1161–1201.

French, Eric, Jones, John and McGee, Rory. 2023. "Why Do Retired Households Draw Down Their Wealth So Slowly?" *Journal of Economic Perspectives*, 37 (4): 91–114.

Lerner, Josh and Nanda, Ramana. 2020. "Venture Capital's Role in Financing Innovation: What We Know and How Much We Still Need to Learn." *Journal of Economic Perspectives*, 34 (3): 237–261.

PART III
MONETARY ECONOMICS

MONEY AND BANKING

MONEY AND THE ECONOMY

Many things can serve as money. Examples include bricks of tea in ancient China, livestock in early societies, salt in ancient Rome, shell beads by Native Americans, and whale teeth in Fiji. As long as members of society assign value to the item and accept it as payment, the item exists as money. In different periods of time and locations around the world, metals such as copper, gold, iron, and silver have served as money. Even leather and stone have served as money. The point is that, throughout history, money has taken different forms.

In modern economies, money is anything that a society accepts for the payment of goods, services, and debt. For centuries, economies have used currency and coins. But for an item to serve as money, all of the buyers and sellers in the economy must accept the item as money. The market must establish its value. It must be used as a standardized form of exchange. The item must be divisible, so consumers receive change. Individuals must be able to use the money for economic transactions, so it must be easy to carry and convey.

Today, electronic money is used for common transactions, moving from employers to banks to retail establishments. This digital form of exchange is the best modern example of *fiat money*, which is money without intrinsic value but is classified as legal tender. In the economy, money is so important that it is necessary to identify its functions, the characteristics of the money supply, how banks create money, the money multiplier, constraints on money creation, and the rise of digital currency.

DOI: 10.4324/9781003678700-10

FUNCTIONS OF MONEY

For a well-functioning economy, money facilitates economic transactions, making it unique as a commodity. First, money serves as a
medium of exchange. Consumers use money to purchase goods and
services. The existence of money avoids barter, when individuals
exchange goods and services for other goods and services. The problem with barter is the difficulty of establishing value. The exchange
of food for clothing may seem reasonable, but one item may have
more value than the other. Across all forms of exchange, a barter
economy is not practical. It requires a *double coincidence of wants*,
when a buyer and a seller each have an item that the other wants. In
reality, consumers may not have the items that create a context for a
transaction. When money serves as a medium of exchange, transactions do not require a double coincidence of wants.

Second, money serves as a *store of value*. Money lasts, facilitating
the process of saving. When individuals save money, they use it to
buy future goods and services. Other commodities, including
stocks, bonds, mutual funds, art, and real estate, store value. Over
time, the commodities may increase in value. The reason that
money serves a unique position in the economy is that individuals
must convert commodities into cash in order to make future purchases. But the process creates transaction costs. Some commodities, such as art and real estate, create significant transaction costs.
As a result, money has the highest degree of liquidity, serving
individuals in the process of exchange. Stocks, bonds, and mutual
funds have high degrees of liquidity, but they experience a transaction cost in the process of conversion into cash. In addition, the
financial market may set lower values for stocks, bonds, and mutual
funds, increasing their market risk. In the absence of inflation,
money does not decrease in value.

Third, money serves as a *unit of account*, a standard unit of measurement. The economy uses money to establish value for goods,
services, and assets. In the absence of this function, it would not be
possible to establish a common unit of measurement for the variety
of items available for purchase. But this function is crucial for
consumers and producers alike. Money creates the dollar value of
costs, prices, and profits. By existing as a unit of account, money
reduces the exposure of economic agents to relative price risk.

MONEY SUPPLY

By serving as a medium of exchange, store of value, and unit of account, money facilitates exchange, bringing together buyers and sellers in the marketplace. But how much money exists in the economy? As a matter of identification, a country's central bank measures the money supply. In addition, the central bank oversees the monetary system. In the United States (US), the Federal Reserve System assumes this role. The central bank develops and records different monetary aggregates, updating the measures with the evolution of the monetary system. The narrowest definition of money, M1, includes currency in circulation (banknotes and coins), demand deposits in banks (checking accounts), traveler's checks, and other accounts with check-writing capabilities. As a broader definition of the money supply, M2 includes M1, money market deposit accounts, savings deposits, shares in money market mutual funds, and small-denomination (less than $100,000) time deposits. While economic agents may draw on M1 instantaneously, the assets in M2 are accessible. In the US, trillions of dollars' worth of M1 and M2 exist in the economy. When economists refer to the money supply in their analyses of the monetary system, they normally refer to the M1 definition. But when economists refer to economic indicators and the state of the economy, they use M2, adjusted for inflation. While the trends for M1 and M2 may deviate, they normally move in tandem. In the following discussion of money creation, the money supply means M1.

HOW BANKS CREATE MONEY

Banks and the money supply facilitate economic activity. The primary purpose of banks is to transfer money from savers to borrowers. By accepting deposits and loaning money to economic agents, banks and other financial institutions have the ability to create money. The process is important in understanding how the economy experiences economic growth. Banks and other financial institutions offer a variety of services, including ATMs, checking accounts, loans, safe deposit boxes, and savings accounts. Of these services, checking accounts are the most important. They are demand deposits, because the balances are due on demand.

FRACTIONAL RESERVES

The M1 definition of the money supply includes currency in circulation and demand deposits in banks. Checking accounts allow banks and other financial institutions to create money by making loans to economic agents. The key is the existence of *fractional reserve banking*. In this system, banks must keep a fraction of the deposits on hand in the form of reserves. They can lend the rest of the money. The result is the creation of new deposits, which increases the money supply. In a fractional reserve banking system, banks do not have to keep the entire amount of their deposits in reserve. When an individual deposits money, the bank must keep the *required reserves* on hand. By definition, required reserves are the amount of money the bank must keep as a percentage of the deposits made by customers. As a form of monetary policy, the central bank sets the required reserve ratio (RRR), the percentage of deposits that banks must hold:

$$Required\, reserves\, =\, (RRR)\,(deposits)$$

If banks do not keep all of the deposits on hand, why does the system work? What prevents a run on the banks, when all of the banks' customers withdraw their money? The system works because the reserve requirement is sufficient to meet the demand for withdrawals. That is, economic agents want to keep money in the banking system, viewing it as a safe and efficient way to maintain access to their money. As long as the economy is stable, the banking system provides enough funds to depositors, and economic agents maintain their faith in the system, fractional reserve banking works. But the central bank must regulate the system, making sure that banks meet their reserve requirement and ensure liquidity in the economy.

Banks loan money for business investments and consumer purchases. Examples of the former include business acquisitions, commercial real estate, and equipment expenditures. Examples of the latter include automobile loans, mortgages, and home equity lines of credit. When individuals deposit money, banks lend most of it to businesses and households. This is how banks make money. The borrowers must pay the loans back plus interest. The reason that banks satisfy the demand for withdrawals is that banks have many customers. In a stable banking system, the customers want to keep money in banks, withdrawing it when necessary.

A run on the bank occurs when many depositors simultaneously want to withdraw their money. They may fear insolvency of the bank and want access to their deposits. The process could lead to the failure of the bank if the bank cannot meet its obligations. During the Great Depression, several of these examples occurred. To ensure against the possibility, the central bank oversees commercial bank holidays, deposit insurance, and regulation. Despite the risk, fractional reserve banking serves as an effective method of money creation.

THE PROCESS OF MONEY CREATION

Through loan activity, the banking system alters the money supply. But banks create money by lending their *excess reserves*, the funds that exceed the reserve requirement:

$$Excess\,reserves\,=\,reserves\,-\,required\,reserves.$$

By loaning money, banks create demand deposits. After making the loans, the money is eventually deposited in the original bank or other banks. The banks maintain some of the deposits in the form of reserves, making new loans. The process continues until all of the excess reserves are loaned in the banking system. The money supply increases, because demand deposits are a part of M1. An illustration of this process uses a stylized version of the bank balance sheet (Figure 7.1). The stylized balance sheet ignores the capital requirements necessary to start a bank.

Bank assets include reserves and loans. The reserves are considered assets because they are the funds from deposits. The loans are considered assets because the borrowers must pay the money back to the bank. The deposits are liabilities because the bank must facilitate

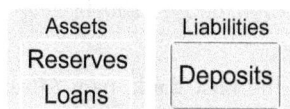

Assets	Liabilities
Reserves	Deposits
Loans	

Figure 7.1 Stylized bank balance sheet

withdrawals. In the simplified version of the banking process, when deposits occur, banks either put the money in reserves or loan the money to economic agents. The same way that individuals and businesses have accounts with commercial banks, the commercial banks have accounts with the central bank. When checks clear, the central bank transfers reserves from one bank to another.

AN EXAMPLE OF MONEY CREATION

In transaction (a), the central bank purchases $500,000 in bonds from a bond dealer. The bond dealer deposits the money in the First Bank. On the asset side of the balance sheet, the First Bank's reserves increase. On the liabilities side, the deposits increase:

First Bank

(a) Reserves (+$500,000)   (a) Deposits (+$500,000)

Because demand deposits rise, the money supply (M1) increases. After the transaction, the First Bank determines the required reserves. If the central bank sets the RRR = 10 percent of deposits, the required reserves are:

$$Required\,reserves = (RRR)\,(deposits)$$
$$= (0.10)\,(\$500,000) = \$50,000.$$

Central bank regulation limits commercial bank lending to the level of excess reserves. The reserve requirement limits the bank's deposit-creation (lending) potential:

$$Excess\,reserves = reserves - required\,reserves =$$
$$\$500,000 - \$50,000 = \$450,000.$$

In transaction (b), the First Bank loans $450,000 to a local business (Smartphone Store) by writing a check to the business, paying for the loan with its reserves:

First Bank

(a) Reserves (+$500,000)	(a) Deposits (+$500,000)
(b) Reserves (-$450,000)	
(b) Loans (+$450,000)	

Total Effects

Reserves (+$50,000)	Deposits (+$500,000)
Loans (+$450,000)	

By loaning money to the Smartphone Store, the First Bank injects money into the economy. After the transaction, the bank's required reserves do not change:

$$Required\,reserves = (RRR)\,(deposits)$$

$$= (0.10)\,(\$500,000) = \$50,000.$$

But the First Bank's excess reserves change:

$$Excess\,reserves = reserves - required\,reserves$$

$$= \$50,000 - \$50,000 = \$0.$$

Because the excess reserves equal zero, the First Bank cannot loan more money.

In transaction (c), the Smartphone Store deposits $450,000 in the Second Bank. For the transaction, the central bank transfers the reserves from the First Bank to the Second Bank:

Second Bank

(c) Reserves (+$450,000)	(c) Deposits (+$450,000)

Both deposits and the money supply (M1) increase. The Second Bank's required reserves are:

$$Required\, reserves = (RRR)\,(deposits)$$

$$= (0.10)\,(\$450,000) = \$45,000.$$

The Second Bank's excess reserves are:

$$Excess\, reserves = reserves - required\, reserves =$$

$$\$450,000 - \$45,000 = \$405,000.$$

Because of the excess reserves, the Second Bank can lend $405,000.

In transaction (d), the Second Bank loans $405,000 to a local business, the Grocery Store, by writing a check to the business. The Second Bank pays for the loan by drawing down its reserves at the central bank:

Second Bank

(c) Reserves (+$450,000)	(c) Deposits (+$450,000)
(d) Reserves (-$405,000)	
(d) Loans (+$405,000)	

Total Effects

Reserves (+$45,000)	Deposits (+$450,000)
Loans (+$405,000)	

By loaning money to the Grocery Store, the Second Bank injects money into the economy. After the transaction, the bank's required reserves do not change:

$$Required\, reserves = (RRR)\,(deposits)$$

$$= (0.10)\,(\$450,000) = \$45,000$$

But the First Bank's excess reserves change:

$$Excess\, reserves = reserves - required\, reserves$$

$$= \$45,000 - \$45,000 = \$0.$$

Because the excess reserves equal zero, the Second Bank cannot loan more money.

In transaction (e), the Grocery Store deposits $405,000 in the Third Bank:

Third Bank

(c) Reserves (+$405,000)   (c) Deposits (+$405,000)

Because demand deposits increase, the money supply rises. Two questions emerge. How much money can the Third Bank lend? The answer is the amount equal to the excess reserves. In the banking system, how long will the money-creating process last? When all of the reserves injected into the economy are held by commercial banks as required reserves, the process ends. No more excess reserves exist. As a result, the commercial banks do not loan more money.

In the process of deposit expansion, the banking system lends a multiple of the original $500,000 deposit in the First Bank. In each round of lending, the money supply increases. What is the value of the total deposit-creation potential of the banking system? One way to answer the question is to continue the example until all of the excess reserves are gone. This is a long process. Fortunately, another way exists: the application of the money multiplier.

MONEY MULTIPLIER

The *money multiplier* is the amount of money that the banking system generates with each dollar of reserves. The money multiplier demonstrates how the banking system alters the money supply by a multiple of the original level of excess reserves. In equation form, economists define the money multiplier in the following manner:

$$Money\,multiplier\,=\,\frac{1}{RRR}$$

If the RRR = 10 percent, the calculation is:

$$Money\,multiplier\,=\,\frac{1}{0.10}\,=\,10$$

The deposit creating potential of the banking system equals the money multiplier times the initial excess reserves:

$$Deposit\ creation\ potential\ of\ the\ banking\ system$$

$$= (money\ multiplier)\ (initial\ excess\ reserves)$$

$$= (10)\ (\$450,000)$$

$$= \$4,500,000$$

The example demonstrates that a bank may loan money equal to its excess reserves. But the banking system creates money by a multiple of the original excess reserves. In the process, the central bank has two roles. First, it increases the money supply by injecting money into the banking system. In the example, the central bank initiates the process by purchasing bonds from a bond dealer. The bond dealer deposits the money in the First Bank. Second, the central bank sets the RRR and the money multiplier. The monetary policy impacts the deposit creating potential of the banking system.

CONSTRAINTS ON MONEY CREATION

Although banks create money by lending their excess reserves, several constraints exist:

- Central bank policy
- Internal risk management
- Liquidity and solvency
- Market forces
- Profitability requirements of the commercial bank
- Regulatory requirements of the central bank
- Willingness of economic agents to borrow

The central bank implements monetary policy, which alters the money supply and interest rates. When the central bank injects money into the banking system, interest rates fall. When the central bank takes money out of the banking system, interest rates rise. The changes influence the availability and cost of new loans. Lower interest rates decrease the cost of borrowing, encouraging both borrowing and lending. Higher interest rates increase the cost of borrowing, discouraging both borrowing and lending. In the broader economy, changes in interest rates impact consumption, economic growth, financial stability, inflation, and investment.

Internal risk management dictates that banks must evaluate the risk of new loans. When managing their balance sheets, banks assess whether the loans to economic agents offer an acceptable level of risk. Do businesses, households, and individuals have sufficient credit scores? Do they have the necessary incomes to make monthly payments? Are there economic factors that complicate the loans? These and other questions inform the process.

Banks maintain liquidity and solvency. To meet their obligations, they must have access to a sufficient amount of liquidity. When the assets exceed the liabilities, banks are solvent. But if banks cannot meet their obligations to borrowers and depositors, they become insolvent. What factors increase the risk of insolvency? Insolvency may occur if banks hold a large percentage of nonperforming loans. In this case, the borrowers cannot maintain their monthly payments. Insolvency may also occur if banks do not have enough liquid assets to process payments to businesses, customers, financial institutions, or other banks. If a bank is failing, it may borrow money from commercial banks or the central bank, although restrictions exist. If failure occurs, federal or state regulators close the bank. In the US, the Federal Deposit Insurance Corporation (FDIC) secures deposits up to $250,000 per person.

Because the volatility in product, factor, and financial markets complicates economic planning, market forces constrain bank lending. Bank loans fluctuate according to the business cycle, increasing during expansions and decreasing during contractions. The reason is that, when the production of output is rising, more income flows to economic agents. Bank lending favors this outcome, because businesses, households, and individuals experience higher levels of prosperity. The demand for credit rises. In contrast, during contractions, banks are more cautious, reducing their lending activity. Even though the procyclical behavior of lending is a function of the business cycle, it amplifies economic fluctuations. An over-extension of credit during periods of growth leads to asset bubbles, when assets are overvalued according to economic fundamentals. A decline in the extension of credit during recessions exacerbates economic downturns.

The profitability requirement constrains the process of lending. When banks lend, the objective is to experience a profit from the transaction. When borrowers are in good standing, they make regular payments of principal and interest. Banks profit from the arrangement. If lending is stable and profitable, banks have the ability to loan money. If lending is risky and unprofitable, banks are limited in their ability to make new loans and expand the money supply. Bank profitability is a function of macroeconomic conditions and market forces. When these factors are favorable, banks are in a position to profit from the process of lending.

The regulatory requirements of the central bank constrain lending activity. Banks must maintain financial capital, which is bank equity, net worth, or the difference between total assets and total liabilities. Regulators measure this requirement by comparing the ratio of equity to assets. In addition, banks must maintain their reserve requirement. Meeting the reserve requirement means holding a specific percentage of deposits as reserves. To satisfy the requirement, banks keep money in their vaults or accounts with the central bank. For practical reasons, banks choose to keep a larger percentage of money with the central bank. Banks use the money in their vaults to meet daily transactions. If banks do not meet their reserve requirement, they borrow either from other banks or from the central bank's discount window.

The willingness of economic agents to borrow money is a function of several factors, including the availability of loans, creditworthiness, economic conditions, existing debt, income, and interest rates. During periods of growth, when banks are willing to loan money, economic agents are likely to borrow. As the level of creditworthiness rises, more borrowing occurs. When the unemployment rate rises, less borrowing occurs. As debt increases, economic agents are less likely to borrow money. The change in income is positively correlated with borrowing activity. But the change in interest rates is negatively correlated with borrowing activity.

THE RISE OF DIGITAL CURRENCY

Digital currency facilitates electronic forms of exchange. Different names include cybercash, digital money, electronic currency, or electronic money. Because of its electronic status, economic agents and financial institutions cannot store it like cash or coins. But when it serves as a medium of exchange, digital currency facilitates economic activity.

Economic agents use digital currency with cards, computers, smartphones, and wiring systems to transfer money. Additional examples include paychecks sent to individuals with digital wallets instead of bank accounts, digital currencies issued by central banks for domestic residents without banking networks, and digital coins. A challenge exists when digital currency is not universally accepted as a medium of exchange.

The benefits of digital currency are accessibility, the decentralized attribute, efficiency and speed, privacy, and a reduction in transaction costs. With accessibility, anyone with an internet connection may use digital currency. The decentralized nature of the currency means that it is more immune to government interference and manipulation. Because of its electronic status, digital currency is faster in satisfying economic transactions than traditional currency and coins.

Compared to traditional currencies, the lower transaction costs from obtaining, storing, and spending digital currency increase the demand. But until regulatory platforms oversee the application of digital currencies, decentralization causes problems, including cyberattacks, faulty algorithms, fraud, outages, and technical issues. Four types of digital currency exist (Table 7.1).

Central bank digital currency (CBDC), an exploratory form of money, exists as an alternative currency. The central bank regulates

Table 7.1 Types of digital currency

Type	Description
Central bank digital currency	Digital form of an economy's official currency
Cryptocurrency	Digital currency used in a computer network that does not rely on a banking system for maintenance and operation
Stablecoins	Type of cryptocurrency in which the value is pegged to another asset, such as gold or a fiat currency
Virtual currency	Digital representation of currency that exists electronically

the currency, facilitating secure payments, especially the payments that cross borders. CBDC broadens the reach of financial services, especially for the individuals without access to the banking system. In the digital economy, CBDC exists as a modern alternative to traditional currency, providing a method for the monetary system to evolve with the digital economy. The payment system offers a resilient method to undertake transactions using a digital ledger. The benefits of the system are bypassing credit checks, eliminating liquidity risks, and fostering economic transactions. The costs are acceptance by the public, operational expenses, regulatory oversight, and the technological infrastructure.

Cryptocurrency serves as a medium of exchange, created and stored electronically on a *blockchain*. The latter is a recording system maintained on computers in a peer-to-peer network. A blockchain shares information across a network of users. *Bitcoin*, an early form of cryptocurrency, generated by a computational system, is independent of central banking. As a digital currency, bitcoin facilitates online payments. For a network of users, it exists in a digital record of transactions. The system guards against the concentration of power, rewarding honest users. It develops a path for the creation of money and provides a public history of transactions. For any form of money, scarcity prescribes value. Bitcoin creates scarcity. To provide an incentive for the bookkeeping system, bitcoin issues new currency at a controlled pace. It is used by businesses and consumers and serves as a method to purchase goods and services, including charitable donations, commodities, and travel. Economic agents start bitcoin accounts without transaction costs or vetting processes. As an adaptable, flexible, and private form of currency, bitcoin, like other cryptocurrencies, exists in an alternative payment system.

Stablecoins are unique forms of cryptocurrency. They are pegged in value to other assets, such as fiat currencies, financial instruments, or gold. The idea is to maintain a stable price. In different blockchain financial services, stablecoins exist as digital currencies. Individuals use them for purchasing. The problem is that, even though stablecoins are pegged to the value of other assets, the market may set a lower value for the assets, introducing volatility. But the benefits include cost-effective transactions, international monetary transfers, and the provision of liquidity in cryptocurrency markets.

Virtual currency, an unregulated form of digital currency, is issued by specific developers. It is used for electronic payments. Transacted in both computer and mobile frameworks, virtual currency exists in specific networks. There are two types. Closed virtual currencies operate in private networks. Economic agents cannot convert closed virtual currencies into fiat currencies or other virtual currencies. Open virtual currencies operate in open networks. Economic agents convert them into fiat currencies or other virtual currencies. The benefits of virtual currency include the completion of digital transactions, elimination of financial intermediaries, and existence of repositories of value. The costs include hackers, a lack of regulation, and volatility.

KEY TERMS

bitcoin
blockchain
digital currency
double coincidence of wants
excess reserves
fiat money
fractional reserve banking
medium of exchange
money multiplier
required reserves
store of value
unit of account

FURTHER READING

Böhme, Rainer, Christin, Nicolas, Edelman, Benjamin and Moore, Tyler. 2015. "Bitcoin: Economics, Technology, and Governance." *Journal of Economic Perspectives*, 29 (2): 213–238.

Fornasari, Massimo. 2023. "On Money: A Brief Intellectual Interpretation." *The Journal of European Economic History*, 52 (1): 183–207.

Senner, Richard and Sornette, Didier. 2019. "The Holy Grail of Crypto Currencies: Ready to Replace Fiat Money?" *Journal of Economic Issues*, 53 (4): 966–1000.

8

MONEY AND INFLATION

MOVIE ECONOMICS

In the 1890s, people started going to the movies. The first film screening occurred in 1896 in New York City. The same year, the first storefront theater opened in New Orleans. In 1905, the first theater dedicated to motion pictures opened in Pittsburgh. During the first two decades of the twentieth century, inexpensive movie theaters called Nickelodeons spread throughout the United States (US). By the 1920s, people flocked to the movies, enjoying the entertainment and social connection. With a growing economy, household incomes were rising. The movies offered an opportunity for people to connect with other members of society. A higher level of disposable income led to new forms of leisure, and the movie industry took advantage of the trend.

In 1925, the price of a ticket to see a movie was $0.25. In current dollars, what was the value of the movie ticket? To answer the question, consider that, in 1925, the Consumer Price Index was equal to 18, with 1982–1984 serving as the base year of 100. One hundred years later, in 2025, the CPI was equal to 320. To estimate the change in value for the 100-year period, the CPI inflator is equal to $320/18 = 17.78$. Multiplying by 100, the price of goods and services increased by 1,778 percent during the period. Using the inflator, the price of a 1925 movie ticket in 2025 dollars = ($0.25)(17.78) = $4.44. But in 2025 the actual price of a movie ticket in the United States was $10.00 on average. Considering the increasing value of the dollar, moviegoers in 1925 experienced a lot of value for their entertainment.

DOI: 10.4324/9781003678700-11

Inflation, a general increase in the price level, seems like a natural economic phenomenon. It is true that the annual price level normally increases. But in the US, there were periods in the 1920s and 1930s when the price level fell. Deflation also occurred in earlier periods, including the 1880s and 1890s. Deflation existed in the early decades in the twentieth century because of a reduction in the money supply and the Great Depression. Deflation occurred in the later decades of the nineteenth century because of higher levels of productivity and lower transportation costs.

Among different countries, international data demonstrate a wide variation for price-level changes. During the twentieth century, France and the United Kingdom experienced periods of inflation and deflation, including a falling price level during the Great Depression and a rising price level during the global oil shocks of the 1970s. In the 1950s, China experienced a relatively stable rate of inflation, but then output decreased, the price level increased, and the economy stagnated. Some countries, including Germany in the 1920s, Hungary in the 1940s, and Zimbabwe in the 2000s, experienced *hyperinflation*, a rapid and unrestrained increase in the price level. This major economic problem led to a decrease in purchasing power, economic and social instability, and a loss of confidence.

The point is that countries have different economic histories, and their outcomes reflect this reality. This century, the inflation rate in many developed countries remained stable until the aftermath of the coronavirus pandemic, in the 2020s, when the price level rose because of disruptions in global supply chains.

In the long run, what determines the level of inflation? Economists often argue that the rate of growth of the money supply serves as an important determinant. In the eighteenth century, the economist and philosopher David Hume (1711–1776) said that a moderate increase in the money supply supported economic growth in the short term. But in the long term the change in the money supply impacted the price level and not variables such as employment or output. Because inflation trends impact economic activity, this chapter discusses the classical theory of inflation, monetary equilibrium, the quantity theory of money, velocity, the Fisher effect, and the outcomes of inflation.

CLASSICAL THEORY OF INFLATION

The classical theory of inflation is named because of its roots with the earliest economists, including Adam Smith (1723–1790) and David Ricardo (1772–1823). The theory posits a direct association between monetary growth and the price level. (It is important to note that there are other factors that cause inflation, such as demand-pull inflation and cost-push inflation, but these short-term factors are addressed in the chapter on aggregate demand and supply.) In this chapter, an increase in the money supply, all else equal, leads to a decrease in the value of money. As an example, suppose the price of a movie ticket doubles. If people are willing and able to pay more money for this form of entertainment, what is the implication? First, the moviegoers may experience more pleasure from the movies. The quality may increase. Second, the pleasure from watching movies may stay the same, but the value of money may fall. The increase in price, in other words, may link to a change in the value of money.

When the Consumer Price Index or another price index rises, the prices of specific goods and services increase. In the 2020s, while the rate of inflation growth was rising, common price increases applied to gasoline, groceries, entertainment, and many other goods and services.

Even though this information provides a useful context to ana-lyze economic activity, general trends are more important in mac-roeconomics. Inflation impacts the economy as a whole. It is associated with the economy's medium of exchange.

The economist Gregory Mankiw notes that it is possible to view the price level in two ways. We may view it as the price of a market basket of goods and services. When the market basket becomes more expensive, consumers pay more money for the items they purchase. But we may also consider the price level as the value of money. When the price level changes, the value of money moves in the opposite direction. When the price level increases, the value of money decreases: money buys fewer goods and services.

When linking the price level to the value of money, P refers to a price index, such as the Consumer Price Index, Producer Price Index, or GDP deflator. In this context, the number of dollars necessary to purchase the market basket of goods and services equals P. In effect, \$1 purchases a quantity of goods and services equal to $1/P$. While P measures the price of goods and services in terms of money, $1/P$ measures the value of money in terms of goods and services.

Consider a simplified economy with one service. Consumers purchase tickets to see the movies, but P changes. If the price of a movie ticket is \$10.00, the value of a dollar $(1/P)$ is one-tenth of a movie. If the price of a movie ticket doubles, the value of a dollar decreases to one-twentieth of a movie. Because the economy has thousands of goods and services that consumers normally purchase, macroeconomists use a price index instead of the price of one service. But the idea is the same. When the price level increases, the value of money decreases.

MONETARY EQUILIBRIUM

The link between the price level and the value of money means a change in the former leads to a difference in the latter. But in a given moment, what determines the value of money? Like other markets in the economy, the answer is supply and demand. In this case, it is the supply of and demand for money. Moving forward, it is important to consider each side of the market.

SUPPLY OF MONEY

The central bank and the banking system determine the supply of money. The central bank may increase or decrease the money supply. When the central bank increases the money supply, it buys bonds in the open market, injects money into the banking system, and decreases interest rates. When the central bank decreases the money supply, it sells bonds in the open market, receives money in exchange, and increases interest rates. If economic agents deposit the money in banks, the banks hold the required reserves and lend the excess reserves. The money multiplier then transforms the initial deposits into a larger effect on the economy. In summary, the supply-side factors include:

- Central bank policy
- Lending from the commercial banking system

DEMAND FOR MONEY

The demand for money is a function of the level of wealth that economic agents want to hold in liquid form. Several determinants exist. Higher incomes lead to more savings and economic transactions, increasing the demand for money. If ATMs are readily available, economic agents hold more money in their wallets. If they rely on credit cards, they hold less money in their wallets. As interest rates rise, the demand for money falls, as economic agents increase their financial investments. The amount of money that economic agents hold also depends on the prices of goods and services. When the prices rise, the value of money falls, so they hold more money in their wallets and checking accounts. They demand a larger quantity of money to purchase output. In summary, the demand-side factors include:

- Income
- Availability of ATMs
- Reliance on credit cards
- Interest rates
- Average price level

EQUILIBRIUM IN THE MONEY MARKET

A market equilibrium exists when supply is in balance with demand. With respect to money, what ensures this outcome? The answer depends on the time horizon. The discussion in Chapter 6 on the loanable funds market demonstrates that the interest rate plays an important role. If a market imbalance occurs, the interest rate adjusts to move the market to equilibrium. For example, if the quantity supplied of loanable funds is greater than the quantity demanded for loanable funds, the interest rate decreases until the market reaches an equilibrium. But what happens in the long run? In the long run, the overall price level establishes an equilibrium between the supply of money and demand for money (Figure 8.1).

At the equilibrium value of money, the quantity of money supplied balances the quantity of money demanded. In the figure, four characteristics are important. First, the horizontal axis displays the quantity of money. Second, the vertical axis on the left displays the value of

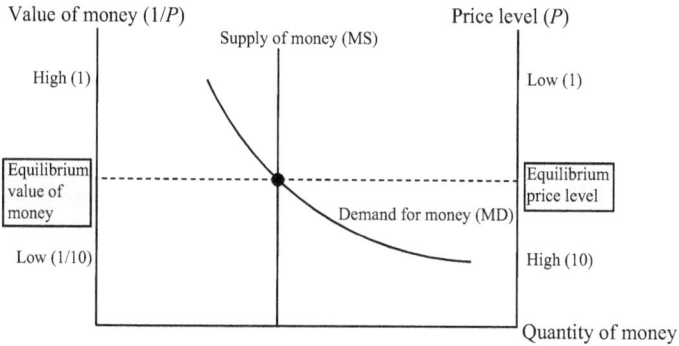

Figure 8.1 Equilibrium value of money

money $(1/P)$. The vertical axis on the right displays an inverted price level (P). When the price level equals 10, the value of money equals $\frac{1}{10}$. Third, the vertical supply curve reflects the fixed supply of money. Assume the central bank determines the money supply, independent of the interest rate or price level. Fourth, the downward-sloping demand curve demonstrates an inverse relationship between the value of money and quantity demanded of money. When the value of money rises because of a lower price level, the quantity demanded of money falls, reflecting that fact that economic agents do not hold as much money in their wallets or checking accounts.

QUANTITY THEORY OF MONEY

The curves in the figure are the supply of and demand for money. But they may shift. For example, if the economy is in the contractionary phase of the business cycle, the central bank may decide to increase the money supply by purchasing bonds in the open market. The policy injects money into the banking system. What is the result? How does the policy impact monetary equilibrium? The policy shifts the supply curve rightward from MS_0 to MS_1 (Figure 8.2). The result is a movement from equilibrium point *a* to *b*, decreasing the value of money from $\frac{1}{4}$ to $\frac{1}{7}$, but increasing the price level from 4 to 7. That is, when the central bank injects money into the banking system, money is more plentiful, the value of money declines, and the price level increases.

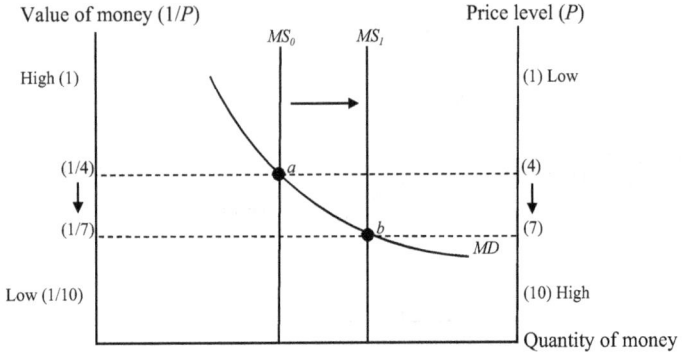

Figure 8.2 Increase in the supply of money

CHANGES IN THE MONEY SUPPLY AND VALUE OF MONEY

Economists use the quantity theory of money to explain the long-term relationship between the money supply and price level. In the long run, the change in the money supply serves as a key determinant of the growth of the price level. In the figures, two observations are important. First, the money supply determines the value of money. When the money supply increases, the value of money decreases. Second, the growth in the quantity of money determines the rate of inflation. When the money supply increases, the price level rises. Together, the factors demonstrate that, in the long run, inflation exists as a monetary phenomenon. But the change in the money supply does not affect real variables in the economy, including employment and output.

How does the process work? How does the economy move from point *a* to *b*? At the original price level at point *a*, individuals have enough money to conduct their economic transactions. But the policy injects money into the economy. At the original price level, the quantity of money demanded is less than the quantity of money supplied. In this case, the banking system loans more money, according to the money multiplier. What do economic agents do with the extra money? They have several options. They may allocate the additional money for houses or property, vehicles, home improvements, educational expenses, or other goods and services. The result of the monetary injection is an increase in the demand for output.

At the same time, the economy's productive capacity does not change. Firms have the same quantity of economic resources and technology. But the higher price level means that, for every transaction, economic agents increase the quantity of money demanded. The reason is that every transaction requires more money. Over time, the economy reaches the new equilibrium at point b, when the quantity of money demanded again equals the quantity of money supplied.

MONEY NEUTRALITY

In the above example of a monetary injection, two important outcomes exist. This section discusses the first outcome. The next section discusses the second outcome.

The first outcome is the *neutrality of money*. In the long run, changes in the money supply alter the price level, but not real variables, such as employment and output. To explain the theory, what is the significance of real variables? Economists classify economic variables in two categories: nominal variables (measured in monetary units) and real variables (measured in physical units). For example, economists classify the income of laborers as a nominal variable, because it is measured in monetary units. But economists classify the quantity of output as a real variable, because it is measured in physical units. Examples of the latter include the quantity of automobiles, pizzas, or smartphones. Nominal GDP exists as a nominal variable because economists measure it with current prices. Real GDP exists as a real variable because economists measure it with constant prices.

Economists classify the difference between nominal and real variables as a classical dichotomy, which means a separation between the two variables. According to classical economic theory, different forces impact nominal and real variables.

This book explains the determination of real variables such as real GDP, real interest rates, and unemployment without a discussion of money. For example, the production of output is a function of economic resources and technology. The balance between the supply of and demand for loanable funds determines the real interest rate. When the real wage exceeds the equilibrium wage, unemployment persists. The supply of money does not affect these variables.

According to classical economic theory, the supply of money affects nominal variables. When the central bank increases the money supply, the price level rises, and the value of money falls. When the central bank decreases the money supply, the price level falls, and the value of money rises.

How accurate is the theory of money neutrality? In actuality, economists argue that, in the short run, changes in the money supply may alter real variables, such as employment and output. If the central bank injects money into the economy, households respond with an increase in the demand for goods and services. At the same time, firms increase their investment. But the theory of money neutrality applies to the long run. Over longer periods of time, such as five to ten years, an increase in the money supply alters the price level, but not real GDP.

EQUATION FOR THE QUANTITY THEORY OF MONEY

In addition to money neutrality, the second important outcome of the quantity theory of money is that economists discuss the theory in terms of an equation. Before introducing the equation, however, consider that, when the central bank injects money into the economy, economists determine the *velocity of money* (V). This is the annual amount the average dollar changes hands. A high velocity indicates a strong economy with more economic activity. A low velocity indicates a weak economy with less economic activity.

The velocity of money equals nominal GDP divided by the money supply. If P is the price level, Y is real GDP, and M is the money supply, the velocity of money is:

$$V = \frac{P \times Y}{M}$$

As an example, suppose an entire economy produces 100 units of output with a per-unit price of $1.00. If the money supply is equal to 20, the velocity of money is:

$$V = \frac{P \times Y}{M} = \frac{\$1 \times 100}{\$20} = 5$$

In the economy, consumers spend $100 on output. But with $20 of money in circulation, each dollar must change hands five times per year. To maintain the balance between the demand for money and the supply of money, the price level adjusts.

By rearranging, economists determine the equation for the quantity theory of money:

$$M \times V = P \times Y$$

The quantity of money times the velocity of money equals the price level times the level of output. With an increase in the money supply, the velocity of money must fall, the price level must rise, or the quantity of output must increase. With the quantity theory, five assumptions exist:

- V is relatively stable
- A change in M by the central bank leads to a proportional change in the nominal value of output $(P \times Y)$
- Y is a function of economic resources and technology, but not money
- Because Y is not a function of M, a change in M impacts P
- When the central bank increases M, inflation occurs

The quantity theory of money requires these five conditions.

THE PROBLEM OF HYPERINFLATION

If economists understand the long-term relationship between the money supply and the price level, why do some countries experience hyperinflation? That is, why do they continue to pump money into the economy if the result is a rapid increase in the price level? The answer is that, in many economic circumstances, governments print money to pay for public spending. Normally, governments raise revenue to pay for roads and highways, education and health care, transfer payments, and other types of expenditure by implementing taxes or borrowing money. But governments may also print money.

As the quantity theory of money demonstrates, the problem with this approach is that, by printing money, the price level rises and the value of money falls. The economist Gregory Mankiw calls the result an inflation tax, or a tax on all economic agents who hold money. While the conditions of the inflation tax vary by country, the conditions are the same. An inadequate level of tax revenue and an inability to borrow money may correspond to a higher level of spending. But hyperinflation follows a large increase in the money supply. A return to a normal rate of inflation does not occur until the government implements fiscal reforms.

THE FISHER EFFECT

The theory of money neutrality means that an increase in the rate of growth of the money supply leads to an increase in the rate of inflation, but not a change in real economic variables. An important outcome relates to interest rates. In macroeconomics, interest rates are important because they serve as the cost of borrowing, reward for saving, and link between savings and investment. But a difference exists between real interest rates and nominal interest rates. Specifically, a nominal interest rate is the market rate, not adjusted for inflation. If an individual has a certificate of deposit (CD), the nominal rate demonstrates how much the money will increase over time. The real interest rate adjusts the nominal rate to reflect purchasing power:

Real interest rate = nominal interest rate − inflation rate

For example, if a CD provides a nominal interest rate equal to 3 percent, but the annual inflation rate equals 4 percent, the individual who owns the CD will experience a decrease in purchasing power: the real interest rate equals -1 percent. Solving for the nominal interest rate yields:

Nominal interest rate = real interest rate + inflation rate

Consider the variables on the right. Chapter 6 explains that the market for loanable funds determines the real interest rate. If the demand for loanable funds increases, the real interest rate rises. In this chapter, the quantity theory of money explains that the growth of the money supply determines the inflation rate. But the theory of money neutrality implies that the growth in the supply of money does not impact real variables, including the real interest rate. As a result, in the long term, when the central bank increases the money supply, the inflation rate and thus the nominal interest rate both rise.

The link between the change in the inflation rate and nominal interest rate is the *Fisher effect*, named after the economist Irving Fisher (1867–1947). The link exists as a long-term, not a short-term, relationship. The reason is that, in the short term, economic agents may not anticipate a rising inflation rate. When a commercial bank issues a CD or loan, it sets the nominal interest rate. If the inflation rate increases, the CD or loan will not reflect the change. But if a higher level of inflation remains, economic agents adjust their expectations. The Fisher effect implies that a change in expected inflation in the long run leads to a change in the nominal interest rate.

OUTCOMES OF INFLATION

While inflation means a general increase in the price level, it does not decrease the purchasing power of consumers if their real wages rise at the same rate. When the real wages of consumers increase at the same rate of inflation, their purchasing power remains constant. If the central bank reduces the rate of increase of the money supply, long-term inflation is low, and the increase in real wages slows. Firms are not compelled to increase output prices, and workers receive smaller wage increases. In this situation, the problem relates to inflation expectations.

If economic agents expect a consistent rise in the price level, such as 1 percent every quarter, economic costs result. The inflation tax alters the amount of money individuals hold. With a higher inflation rate, the nominal interest rate rises, and individuals hold less money as cash and in their checking accounts. A cost results from the process of withdrawing more money. In addition, a higher level of inflation induces firms to increase their prices, which raises operating costs. A change in relative prices impacts sales. Firms sell more output at different times of the year, leading to inefficiencies in the allocation of economic resources. Finally, when inflation is rising, money serves as a less efficient measure of value, complicating financial planning for households and business operations for firms.

In the presence of unexpected inflation, such as when the price level rises due to global supply chain problems or a trade policy that restricts imports, a redistribution of wealth occurs. With loan agreements, the lending institution specifies the nominal interest rate. But unexpected inflation leads to a different real rate of return. If the inflation rate is higher than expected, the debtor repays the loan with less valuable money, at the expense of the creditor. In addition, individuals with fixed pensions suffer from unexpected inflation, if the pensions are fixed in nominal terms.

KEY TERMS

Fisher effect
hyperinflation
neutrality of money
velocity of money

FURTHER READING

Ardakani, Omid. 2023. "The dynamics of money velocity." *Applied Economics Letters*, 30 (13): 1814–1822.

Arthmar, Rogério and Castañeda, Juan. 2024. "Neoclassical economics on the edge: Fisher, Knight, and the theory of interest in the 1930s." *The European Journal of the History of Economic Thought*, 31 (4): 587–607.

Cochrane, John. 2022. "Fiscal Histories." *Journal of Economic Perspectives*, 36 (4): 125–146.

PART IV
CYCLICAL INSTABILITY

AGGREGATE EXPENDITURES

THE POWER OF SPENDING

In 2020, during the early months of the coronavirus pandemic, economic shutdowns, household quarantines, and social distancing increased unemployment for service-sector workers. As the unemployment rate rose, individuals had less money to spend on appliances, beverages, clothing, electronics, food, and other goods and services. The decrease in spending caused a chain reaction, decreasing production, further reducing consumption, and lowering income. During the pandemic, an initial change in consumer demand led to a larger macroeconomic impact on income and output.

The general idea of an economic chain reaction was described by John Maynard Keynes (1883–1946) in *The General Theory of Employment, Interest, and Money* (1936). Keynes, writing during the Great Depression, argued that the government should intervene during economic downturns. If the chain reaction was left unchecked, according to Keynes, the economy would continue to spiral downward. The government's responsibility was to counteract the economic downturn by increasing spending and placing the economy back on the path to economic growth.

During the coronavirus pandemic, the governments of many countries took Keynes' advice, implementing public policies to pump money into their economies, providing resources for households and social programs, and helping the economies recover.

The modern interpretation of Keynesian theory is that, during an economic contraction, the government should play a role in stabilizing the economy. An increase in government spending

DOI: 10.4324/9781003678700-13

boosts consumer demand, leading to an increase in production. Over time, the multiplier effect reduces the unemployment rate and reverses the negative trajectory of the economy.

In macroeconomics, it is important to understand the power of spending and how it multiplies throughout the economy. But some important questions exist. How does the multiplier process work? What are the components of aggregate expenditure? When the economy is contracting, how should governments intervene? These and other questions inform the chapter's topic: aggregate expenditures.

The goal of government spending programs is to put money in the hands of households and businesses. The government has several policy options, including direct forms of expenditure, tax cuts, subsidies, and financial assistance. While a successful policy increases the level of aggregate expenditure, costs exist. The higher level of spending may lead to inflation. It may also lead to an increase in the annual government deficit and overall debt. The future pressure to address the costs may lead to a new round of policy that reverses the economic gains. That is, additional policy may have to slow the price-level increase.

During the 1940s and beyond, Keynesianism, the idea of government intervention with a contracting economy, revolutionized the field of economics. Before the publication of Keynes' epic book, in 1936, classical economists argued that, if economies were left to themselves, they would naturally adjust to economic fluctuations, and return to full employment.

In classical economics, the government's role was to establish the framework for economies to operate, including the administration of the legal system, preservation of competition, and maintenance of national defense. But the classical framework did not argue that the government should guarantee full employment, or intervene during economic slumps. In the classical view, downturns in economic activity were self-correcting. That is, the forces of supply and demand would return the economy to full employment.

In the field of economics, Keynes' analysis turned the perspective away from the classical system. This is the reason that Keynes was the most prominent economist of the twentieth century. Today, the Keynesian perspective is still relevant, focusing on the role of the government during economic downturns. But policy questions remain. To what extent should the government intervene? If the government decides to intervene, what policies should it implement? How long should the intervention last? Because the answers to these questions address cyclical fluctuations, the chapter discusses Say's Law and the circular flow, aggregate expenditures, the simple model of aggregate expenditures, and the full model of aggregate expenditures.

SAY'S LAW AND THE CIRCULAR FLOW

The story begins with Jean-Baptiste Say (1767–1832), a French economist who argued for competition and free trade. In Say's analysis, the act of supplying output generated the income necessary to purchase the output. If businesses produced more goods and services, households would use the additional income to purchase more goods and services.

Using Say's terminology, a merchant could suffer from an abundance of goods in the warehouse, but an economy was unlikely to experience the same outcome. An economy's power of purchasing equaled its annual production. As production rose, the country's national market and purchasing power increased. No sooner was output created, according to Say, than from it emerged a market for other goods and services equal to its value. In this framework, overproduction was impossible: the income from economic activity created a corresponding demand.

Today, the idea is known as *Say's Law*: "supply creates its own demand." The core principle of Say's Law is that supply exists as the underlying factor of the economy. In the circular flow model, the production of goods and services in product markets creates a flow of income to the owners of the factors of production. When the production of output increases, the economy generates more income, giving households the ability to purchase the additional goods and services. The implication is that the economy gravitates toward full employment. The supply and demand sides of the market are in balance. There is no need for government intervention.

Although early economists challenged Say's Law, including Thomas Malthus (1766–1834) and Karl Marx (1818–1883), it became an important position in classical economics, dominating economic thinking until John Maynard Keynes identified a weakness in 1936. As this chapter explains, the weakness in the argument is that, in the short run, the economy may not always gravitate toward full employment. If the economy contracts, a high level of unemployment may persist. The theory of business cycles validates this perspective.

But a certain long-run validity to Say's Law exists. With economic growth, an economy produces more output, generating higher payments to the factors of production. The process increases the demand for output. At the same time, when an economy produces more for the foreign sector, exports rise, and the economy can afford to import more goods and services. In the long run, supply creates its own demand in both domestic and foreign trade.

In the short run, however, cyclical fluctuations move the economy away from full employment. Changes in both the demand and supply sides of the market create this outcome. The problem is that the economy may establish a level of production that differs from full employment, and the position may persist. As a result, the income flowing to the factors of production may be enough to purchase output, but there is no guarantee that the economic agents will spend the money. To understand why, the next section discusses aggregate expenditures, and the potential for a break in the link between output and income.

AGGREGATE EXPENDITURES

Economists determine gross domestic product (GDP) by adding aggregate spending or aggregate income in the economy. On the expenditure side, GDP consists of consumer spending (C), investment (I), government spending (G), and net exports (X − M). With these categories, aggregate expenditures (AE) are equal to:

$$GDP = AE = C + I + G + (X - M)$$

The assumption is that saving is personal saving (S) and not national saving. In economics, S is the level of saving left over after personal consumption and the payment of taxes. The following discussion develops the simple model of aggregate expenditures without government and the foreign sector. These elements are then added to the model.

CONSUMPTION AND SAVINGS

For many countries, such as the United States, consumption expenditure constitutes the largest share of GDP. In the national income accounts, consumption refers to spending on durable goods, non-durable goods, and services. Aggregate consumption normally increases on an annual basis. A decrease in aggregate consumption, when it occurs, reflects a downturn in economic activity.

Households spend most of their income on consumption. Consumption is a function of income (Y). In general, as Y increases, C increases. But consumption does not increase on a dollar-for-dollar basis. Saving occurs. In this framework, $S = Y - C$. That is, households allocate their income to consumption and saving.

This approach differs from the classical explanation of saving. Classical economists argue that the interest rate influences the level of savings. But the Keynesian framework demonstrates that saving is a function of income. Table 9.1 shows a numerical relationship between C, S, and Y. The numbers are in dollars.

The *average propensity to consume* (APC) and *average propensity to save* (APS) serve as important indicators of consumer spending. They help

Table 9.1 Hypothetical consumption, saving, and income data

Income or output (Y)	Consumption (C)	Saving (S)	APC ()	APS ()	MPC ()	MPS ()
6,000	6,500	-500	1.08	-0.08	0.75	0.25
6,400	6,800	-400	1.06	-0.06	0.75	0.25
6,800	7,100	-300	1.04	-0.04	0.75	0.25
7,200	7,400	-200	1.03	-0.03	0.75	0.25
7,600	7,700	-100	1.01	-0.01	0.75	0.25
8,000	8,000	0	1.00	0	0.75	0.25
8,400	8,300	100	0.99	0.01	0.75	0.25
8,800	8,600	200	0.98	0.02	0.75	0.25
9,200	8,900	300	0.97	0.03	0.75	0.25
9,600	9,200	400	0.96	0.04	0.75	0.25
10,000	9,500	500	0.95	0.05	0.75	0.25

economists understand market trends. The APC, which equals consumption divided by income, is a measure of how much income the household allocates for consumption. This is the portion of income that the household does not save. At the aggregate level, a higher value for the APC indicates that households are spending a larger percentage of their income on consumption. A higher value for the APC boosts economic activity.

The APS, which equals saving divided by income, is a measure of how much income the individual allocates for savings. This is the portion of income that the household does not spend. At the aggregate level, a higher value for the APS indicates that households are saving a larger percentage of their income on savings. A higher value for the APS slows economic activity. Because households allocate their income for either consumption or savings, $APC + APS = 1$.

The *marginal propensity to consume* (MPC) and *marginal propensity to save* (MPS) indicate the pattern for consumption and saving when income changes. The MPC, which equals the change in consumption divided by the change in income, demonstrates how much households want to spend when their income rises or falls. If the MPC is relatively high, households are spending a larger portion of additional income on consumption.

The MPS, which equals the change in savings divided by the change in income, demonstrates how much households want to save when their income rises or falls. If the MPS is relatively high, households are saving a larger portion of additional income. Once again, $MPC + MPS = 1$.

Economists study the factors that drive the averages and marginals. With this information, they observe consumer behavior. But they also forecast consumer behavior.

Two forms of consumption exist. First, *autonomous consumption* is the part of consumption that is not dependent on income. Even if households do not experience a flow of income, they still consume goods and services. They finance this expenditure by drawing down savings or borrowing money. The non-income determinants of consumption include:

- Credit: when households obtain credit, they spend more than their current income

- Expectations: when households forecast a positive future, including a pay raise or tax refund, they may consume more goods and services before the money arrives
- Taxes: taxes separate disposable income from total income, so when taxes rise, consumption falls
- Wealth: when the value of assets rises, the household's ability and willingness to consume goods and services increases

Second, a portion of household spending depends on income. When income rises, this portion of consumption increases. In this context, the MPC serves as the important parameter.

With these two forms of consumption, the consumption function is written as:

$$C = a + bY$$

where C = current consumption
a = autonomous consumption; $a > 0$
b = marginal propensity to consume; $0 < b < 1$
Y = income

To analyze the spending behavior of households, economists estimate the numerical values of a and b. How do they estimate the values? Two options exist: looking at historical data for the aggregate economy or surveying households. (For the estimation, keep in mind that a is the spending that does not depend on income, but b is the spending that depends on income.) Assume the information in Table 9.1 is survey data. The first step is to calculate b, the MPC. The table shows that $b = MPC = 0.75$. The second step is to calculate a by choosing a level of income and plugging it into the consumption function. In the table, when $Y = 6,000$, $C = 6,500$. Plugging into the consumption function yields:

$$C = a + bY$$
$$6,500 = a + (0.75)(6,000)$$
$$6,500 = a + 4,500$$
$$a = 2,000$$

With the parameter values, the consumption function is:

$$C = 2,000 + 0.75\,(Y)$$

The consumption function allows economists to advance from an observation of consumer spending to prediction (how much spending will change when income rises or falls). Figure 9.1 facilitates the analysis. Along the 45-degree line, $C = Y$. When the consumption function intersects the 45-degree line, saving equals zero. This point occurs when $C = Y = 8,000$. To the left of the point, dissaving exists, because $C > Y$. To the right of the point, saving exists, because $C < Y$.

Although economists use the consumption function to predict consumer behavior, it may shift. The reason is that economic behavior changes, impacting the level of a and b. For example, if consumers are confident in the future, they may increase their level of autonomous consumption. But the MPC may also rise. Two principles exist:

- If a changes, the consumption function shifts up or down
- If b changes, the consumption function rotates up or down

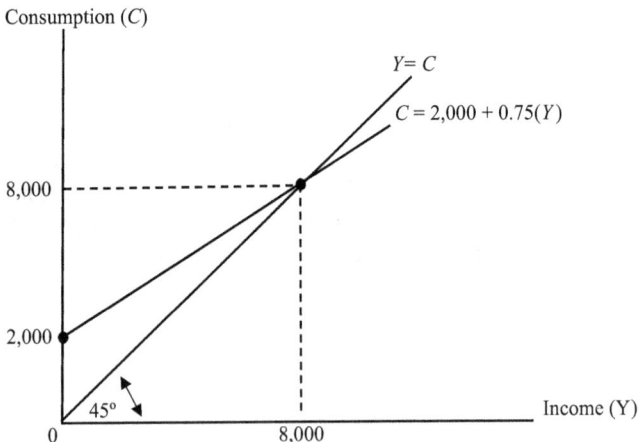

Figure 9.1 Consumption function

INVESTMENT

In the national income accounts, investment refers to business spending on new plant and equipment, changes in business inventories, and new housing starts. The level of new investment spending depends on marginal cost and marginal benefit. To finance new investment opportunities, firms often borrow money. The interest rate is the cost of borrowing. The rate of return on capital serves as the benefit of borrowing. Firms undertake projects when the rate of return exceeds the cost of borrowing.

An inverse relationship exists between investment and the interest rate, which means the investment demand curve slopes downward. But several factors shift investment demand, including capital goods on hand, expectations, operating costs, and technological change. For example, the fewer capital goods a firm has on hand, including existing inventories, the more that firms will make new investments. In this case, investment demand increases, shifting rightward from I_0 to I_1 (Figure 9.2). Overall, investment demand increases in the presence of fewer capital goods on hand, positive future expectations, lower operating costs, or technological advancement.

SIMPLE MODEL OF AGGREGATE EXPENDITURES

Before the inclusion of the government and foreign sector, aggregate expenditure in the simple model consists of the sum of consumer and business spending: $AE = C + I$ (Figure 9.3).

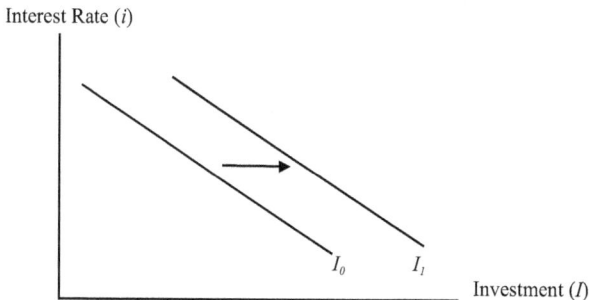

Figure 9.2 Shift in investment demand

Aggregate expenditure (AE)

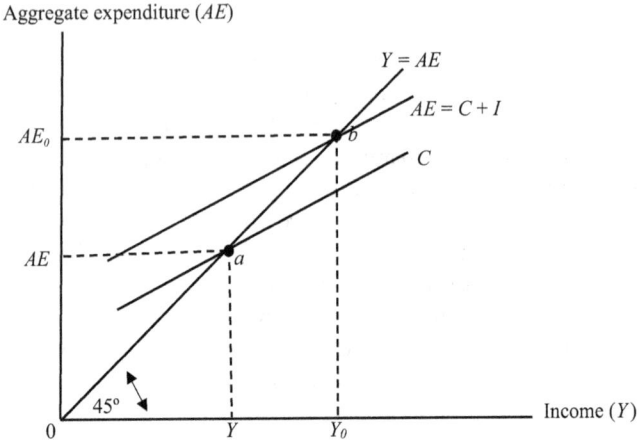

Figure 9.3 Simple model of aggregate expenditure

In the model, what is the macroeconomic equilibrium? The equilibrium is the level of income in which no pressure exists to produce more or less output. At point *a*, $AE > C$, so consumers and businesses want to spend more money. At this point, the economic agents demand more goods and services than the economy produces. As a result, production and income increase, and the economy moves to point *b*. At Y_0, the level of output that economic agents want to buy is equal to the output that firms produce.

To consider the macroeconomic equilibrium from another angle, AE in the simple model equals consumption plus business investment. In equilibrium, income, output, and AE are equal ($Y = AE$). At the same time, income is either spent or saved ($Y = C + S$). Therefore, at equilibrium:

$$C + I = C + S$$

Canceling C on each side yields:

$$I = S$$

At the macroeconomic equilibrium, investment equals savings.

INJECTIONS AND LEAKAGES

What happens when $I \neq S$? When desired investment > desired savings (left of point b), income will rise. When desired investment < desired savings (right of point b), income will fall. What is the implication? *Injections* refer to money that flows into the economy's spending cycle. In the simple model, investment serves as an injection. Injections increase total spending and stimulate economic activity. *Leakages* refer to money that leaves the economy's spending cycle. In the simple model, saving serves as a leak. Leakages decrease total spending.

A useful analogy is a bucket of water. If the flow of water from a faucet into the bucket (injection) equals the flow of water out of the bucket from a hole (leak), the water level (economy) remains the same. But if the leak is greater than injection, the economy shrinks.

MULTIPLIER EFFECT

In the economy, injections and leakages create an overall outcome that exceeds the initial change in spending. The *multiplier effect* means that an initial change in spending leads to a larger change in economic activity. How does the process work? When the $MPC = 0.75$, economic agents allocate 75 percent of additional income to spending and 25 percent to saving. If businesses spend \$1,000 on new equipment and machinery, the firms that produce the capital goods will spend \$750 on raw materials and save \$250. The firms supplying the raw materials will receive \$750 in new income, spending \$562.50 (0.75 x \$750). How long will the process continue? It will continue until the economy exhausts all of the additional spending. The method to calculate the overall level of additional spending is to use the equation for the spending multiplier (k), which is derived from the equation for AE and the consumption function:

$$K = \frac{1}{1 - MPC}$$

When the $MPC = 0.75$, the spending multiplier is:

$$K = \frac{1}{1 - MPC} = \frac{1}{1 - 0.75} = \frac{1}{0.25} = 4$$

Because $MPC + MPS = 1$, another way to write the spending multiplier is:

$$K = \frac{1}{MPS}$$

Table 9.2 provides different values for the MPC, and the corresponding values for k.

For macroeconomists, the framework is useful in forecasting economic activity. They use the spending multiplier to calculate the total change in income (ΔY) that results from an initial change in autonomous investment (ΔI):

$$\Delta Y = (k)(\Delta I)$$

For example, if investment increases by $1,000,000, the $MPC = 0.75$, and $k = 4$, economists forecast the overall change in income and output in the economy as:

$$\Delta Y = (k)(\Delta I) = (4)(\$1,000,000) = \$4,000,000$$

An increase in investment raises equilibrium income by a multiple of the initial injection.

It is important to note, however, that the multiplier works in both directions. In the simple economy, when $k = 4$, a decrease in investment of $1,000,000 will reduce spending by $4,000,000. This is the reason that economists study consumer confidence during recessions. When the economy contracts, income falls. When households withhold money from the cycle of spending, leakages increase. As households increase their savings to hedge

Table 9.2 Expenditure multiplier

MPC	k
0.95	20
0.90	10
0.80	5
0.75	4
0.50	2

against the possibility of losses in employment, the multiplier effect exacerbates the economic downturn. The result is a reduction in income by a multiple of the initial change in spending.

After the onset of the coronavirus pandemic, the multiplier effect is the reason that many governments acted so quickly. The governments knew that if businesses and households decreased their spending, the overall economic impact would be severe. In response, the governments pumped money into the economies, stimulating aggregate expenditures.

FULL MODEL OF AGGREGATE EXPENDITURES

The simple model of aggregate expenditures with household consumption and business investment demonstrates that, at macroeconomic equilibrium, saving equals investment. In addition, an increase in spending leads to a larger change in income and output, according to the multiplier effect. The full model of aggregate expenditures includes the public sector (government spending and taxation) and the foreign sector (exports and imports).

GOVERNMENT SPENDING AND TAXATION

The addition of the public sector means the inclusion of government spending (G) in the aggregate expenditures identity:

$$AE = C + I + G$$

At the federal level, government spending includes discretionary spending (education, national defense, natural resources and environment, research, and transportation), entitlement spending (healthcare, income security, social security), debt payments, and other areas (agriculture and the legal system). The government raises money through taxation (T). Taxation takes many forms, including taxes on income, property, and sales.

With the multiplier effect, a change in aggregate expenditure causes income and output to increase or decrease by the level of spending times the multiplier. The full model includes changes in G and T. For example, if government spending increases by \$5,000,000, the $MPC = 0.75$, and $k = 4$, the overall impact on the economy is:

$$\Delta Y = (k)(\Delta G) = (4)(\$5,000,000) = \$20,000,000.$$

The model maintains macroeconomic equilibrium when injections equal leakages. It does not matter whether the injections come from investment or government expenditure. The key is spending. But how does T impact the economy? The answer is not as simple as the change in government expenditure.

When T changes, money is either pumped into or withdrawn from the economy. When T rises, the government collects money from the economy's spending stream because businesses and households have less money to spend. When T falls, the government injects money into the economy's spending stream because businesses and households have more money to spend.

In the model, taxes exist as a wedge between income and the part of income that is spent (disposable income): $Y_d = Y - T$. Assume taxation exists as a lump-sum payment, eliminating the need to consider the incentive effects of a change in tax rates.

Table 9.3 adds disposable income to the model, reflecting the impact of T. All of the numbers are in dollars. Injections equal investment and government spending $(I + G)$. Leakages now equal saving and taxation $(S + T)$. Equilibrium means that injections equal leakages:

Table 9.3 Equilibrium analysis

Income or output (Y)	Taxes (T)	Disposable income (Y_d)	Consumption (C)	Saving (S)	Investment (I)	Government expenditure (G)
8,000	200	7,800	7,850	-50	200	200
8,200	200	8,000	8,000	0	200	200
8,400	200	8,200	8,150	50	200	200
8,600	200	8,400	8,300	100	200	200
8,800	200	8,600	8,450	150	200	200
9,000	200	8,800	8,600	200	200	200
9,200	200	9,000	8,750	250	200	200
9,400	200	9,200	8,900	300	200	200
9,600	200	9,400	9,050	350	200	200
9,800	200	9,600	9,200	400	200	200
10,000	200	9,800	9,350	450	200	200

$$I + G = S + T$$

In the table, injections = leakages $(I + G = S + T)$ at an income level of 9,000 (shaded). Without the tax, the macroeconomic equilibrium would occur at 9,600, where $S = I + G$ (the 200 from the tax is added to income). The tax decreases equilibrium income by 600. Because the tax reduces consumption spending, the intention of the policy is to reduce income in this manner.

Why does income decrease by 600 and not by 800, which is the value of the tax (200) times the multiplier (4)? In the example, the consumers react to the tax by decreasing their saving. With an $MPC = 0.75$, the tax of 200 is allocated between a decrease in consumption of 150 and a decrease in saving of 50. When the decrease in consumption of 150 is multiplied by $k = 4$, the value of the multiplier, the reduction in income equals 600. In the example, a reduction in saving dampens the effect of the tax on equilibrium income. Consumers withdrew the savings from the stream of spending. But switching the leakages from savings to taxes does not alter the impact on income.

With the full model, the consumption function reflects disposable income:

$$C = a + b(Y_d)$$

or

$$C = a + b(Y - T)$$

A change in either income or taxes alters the level of consumption. But a change in taxation will not have the same effect on equilibrium income as a change in government expenditure or business investment. As a result, economists place the MPC in the numerator of the tax multiplier (z):

$$z = \frac{MPC}{1 - MPC}$$

Table 9.4 compares the numerical values of the spending multiplier (for ΔI and ΔG) and the tax multiplier (for ΔT). No matter the numerical value of the MPC, z is one less than k.

Table 9.4 Spending and tax multipliers

MPC	k	z
0.95	20	19
0.90	10	9
0.80	5	4
0.75	4	3
0.50	2	1

NET EXPORTS

The previous model assumes a closed economy without a foreign sector. Adding the foreign sector means the inclusion of exports and imports:

$$AE = C + I + G + (X - M).$$

The foreign sector impacts AE through net exports: exports minus imports. In the model, X is an injection into the circular flow of economic activity. When the country exports goods and services, foreign economic agents send money into the domestic economy, creating an inward flow of income. But M is a leak out of the circular flow of economic activity. When the country imports goods and services, domestic economic agents send money to foreign economies, creating an outward flow of income. With the inclusion of the foreign sector, the injections equal the leakages:

$$I + G + X = S + T + M.$$

If X rises while the other forms of spending remain the same, equilibrium income increases. But if M rises while the other forms of spending remain the same, equilibrium income decreases. For these reasons, economists consider the trade balance. As Chapter 2 explains, a trade surplus exists when $X > M$. But a trade deficit exists when $X < M$.

The full AE model (Figure 9.4) demonstrates the impact of spending on the economy, creating an equilibrium level of aggregate expenditure ($AE^\star$) and income ($Y^\star$). Investment, government expenditure, and exports increase aggregate income, but savings,

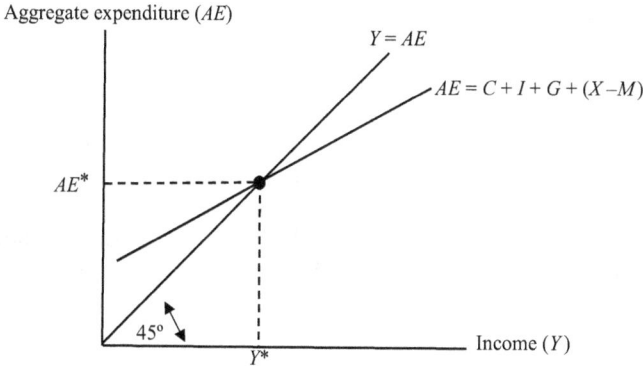

Figure 9.4 Full model of aggregate expenditures

taxes, and imports decrease aggregate income. In addition, the *MPC* and *MPS* mean that consumers spend a portion and save a portion of their additional income. The outcome is a multiplier effect, which magnifies the impact of the initial change in spending on the economy.

RECONSIDERATION OF SAY'S LAW

Keynesian analysis demonstrates the economy needs an injection if it is experiencing an economic contraction, such as the Great Depression of the 1930s, energy shock of 1973–1975, Great Recession of 2007–2009, or coronavirus pandemic of 2020. In the absence of an increase in *AE*, the economy may establish a macroeconomic equilibrium below full employment and remain at that point. The economic downturns of the last century demonstrate the possibility.

According to Keynes, if businesses, consumers, and foreign economic agents are unwilling or unable to spend more money during economic downturns, the government should intervene. That is, the government should inject money into the economy. As this chapter demonstrates, the government may achieve this outcome by increasing *G*, decreasing *T*, or both. The total impact will be a multiple of the initial level of spending.

What does Keynesian analysis mean for Say's Law? In the Keynesian framework, production generates income, but economic agents may not spend the additional income on goods and services. They may save it. If savings increase, leakages out of the spending stream rise, creating the potential for a contracting economy.

In the Keynesian framework, economic agents may or may not spend additional income. That is, the classical case when the economy naturally gravitates to full employment may not hold. This is the general theory. Therefore, a better way to state Say's Law is that "supply creates potential demand."

KEY TERMS

autonomous consumption
average propensity to consume
average propensity to save
injections
leakages
marginal propensity to consume
marginal propensity to save
multiplier effect
Say's Law

FURTHER READING

Béraud, Alain and Numa, Guy. 2018. "Beyond Say's Law: The Significance of J.-B. Say's Monetary Views." *Journal of the History of Economic Thought*, 40 (2): 217–241.

Eichengreen, Barry. 2020. "Keynesian economics: can it return if it never died?" *Review of Keynesian Economics*, 8 (1): 23–35.

Farrell, Henry and Quiggin, John. 2017. "Consensus, Dissensus, and Economic Ideas: Economic Crisis and the Rise and Fall of Keynesianism." *International Studies Quarterly*, 61 (2): 269–283.

AGGREGATE DEMAND AND SUPPLY

MACROECONOMIC OUTCOMES

When economies grow and contract, aggregate expenditures play an important role. According to John Maynard Keynes, the British economist, the spending by consumers, businesses, governments, and foreign buyers serves as a key driver of economic activity. The changes in economic activity that result from these sources of spending determine employment and output. During this century, different economic trends demonstrate this reality.

In many developed countries, the early years of the century were characterized by economic growth. But the Great Recession (2007–2009), caused by banking and housing crises in the United States (US), led to an increase in unemployment, a decrease in production, and a slow recovery. Once industrialized economies stabilized, however, they experienced a decade-long period of expansion, with higher levels of consumer, business, and government spending. In many economies, unemployment reached historical lows, creating an economic environment conducive to economic growth. Economic resources and technological advancements contributed to the growing economies. While the coronavirus pandemic of 2020–2022 slowed the rate of economic growth, economies recovered in a short period of time.

While Keynes' economic analysis focuses on changes in aggregate expenditure as the impetus for business cycles, he did not fully analyze the impact on the price level. Why? Keynes' most important writing occurred during the Great Depression, when economies were characterized by the underutilization of economic resources.

DOI: 10.4324/9781003678700-14

The 1930s included high levels of unemployment. Businesses were not investing in physical capital. As a result, when governments started spending money and putting people to work in programs such as the New Deal, in the US, no upward pressure on the price level existed. Because of unemployment, businesses hired workers without increasing their wages.

In the field of economics, Keynes' fixed-price model led to two important outcomes: the link between aggregate expenditure and economic outcomes; and the foundation of the demand side of macroeconomics. This chapter adds the supply side, establishing a flexible price model. This approach demonstrates that the price level rises when the overall level of demand increases, or the overall level of supply decreases. These factors explain why the price level increased during the early 2020s, after the pandemic. During this period, consumer demand rose after governments pumped money into the economy, and global supply chain bottlenecks reduced market supply.

To discuss these issues, the chapter develops the model of *aggregate demand* (*AD*) and *aggregate supply* (*AS*), focusing on macroeconomic equilibrium. In addition to demonstrating the reasons for a change in the price level, the model shows that, when *AD* decreases or *AS* increases, the price level falls. Finally, the *AD-AS* model explains cyclical fluctuations: when *AD* and/or *AS* shift, the economy deviates from full-employment production.

AGGREGATE DEMAND

The downward-sloping *AD* curve shows the amount of output (real GDP) that consumers want to purchase at different price levels (Figure 10.1). The shape of the *AD* curve is the same as the demand curve for individual goods and services. The individual demand curve slopes downward because of the Law of Demand: when price increases, quantity demanded decreases, ceteris paribus. But there are different reasons for the shape of *AD*.

REASONS FOR THE SHAPE OF AD

The first reason for the shape of *AD* is the *export price effect*. When the home price level falls, domestic goods and services become less

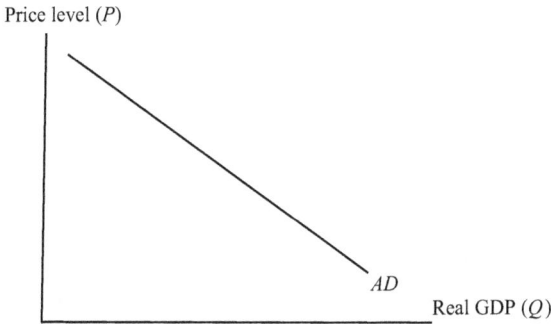

Figure 10.1 AD curve

expensive in the global marketplace. In the global economy, lower prices mean that domestic output is more competitive. The result is that foreign economic agents purchase more domestic products, increasing the home country's exports. An increase in exports raises the demand for domestically produced products. That is, the quantity of output purchased by foreign consumers rises. Because exports are a component of GDP, lower domestic prices result in a higher level of real output.

The second reason for the shape of *AD* is the *interest rate effect*. In this context, the interest rate is the price of borrowing. At one moment in time the quantity of money is fixed. When the price level falls, economic agents demand less money for their transactions. As the demand for money decreases, the cost of borrowing money (interest rate) falls. A declining interest rate leads to an increase in the quantity of investment. The latter outcome increases real GDP.

The third reason for the shape of *AD* is the *wealth effect*. As the price level falls, household wealth rises. But households hold some of their wealth (the total value of household assets minus debts) in the form of financial assets, including stocks, bonds, and mutual funds. When the aggregate price level falls, the purchasing power of the financial assets rises. The increase means that households accelerate their purchasing decisions, increasing the quantity demanded for goods and services. A reduction in the price level leads to an increase in real GDP.

DETERMINANTS OF *AD*

The negative slope of *AD* means that, when the aggregate price level changes, the quantity of real GDP demanded increases or decreases along the *AD* curve. But the curve may shift. The determinants are the components of "ceteris paribus," when everything else is held constant along the *AD* curve. When economists relax the ceteris paribus assumption, the *AD* curve shifts to the right or left.

What are the determinants of *AD*? They are the spending components of GDP, including consumption, investment, government expenditure, and exports (Table 10.1). For example, if consumption expenditure increases because of positive consumer expectations, the *AD* curve increases, shifting to the right. In addition, when the expected rate of return on capital projects increases, investment rises, shifting *AD* to the right. Furthermore,

Table 10.1 Determinants of AD

Determinant	AD increases (shifts right)	AD decreases (shifts left)
Consumer spending		
–Consumer expectations	Improve	Worsen
–Household debt	Decreases	Increases
–Taxes	Decrease	Increase
–Wealth	Increases	Decreases
Investment		
–Business expectations	Improve	Worsen
–Expected return on investments	Increases	Decreases
–Taxes	Decrease	Increase
Government expenditure		
–Discretionary spending	Increases	Decreases
–Mandatory spending	Increases	Decreases
Exports		
–Foreign income	Increases	Decreases
–Exchange rate	Depreciating home currency	Appreciating home currency

when government expenditure rises, *AD* increases, shifting to the right. If foreign income rises or the value of the domestic currency falls, exports increase, raising *AD*. Other factors also increase *AD*.

AGGREGATE SUPPLY

At all price levels, the *AS* curve shows how much output firms produce and sell. Unlike the *AD* curve, the shape of the *AS* curve depends on the time horizon. The long-run aggregate supply (*LRAS*) curve is vertical. But the short-run aggregate supply (*SRAS*) curve slopes upward (Figure 10.2). To analyze short-run economic fluctuations and the difference between short-run and long-run outcomes, it is important to analyze both of the curves.

LONG-RUN AGGREGATE SUPPLY

In the long run, the quantity of output that the economy produces (real GDP) depends on the supply of economic resources (capital, labor, natural resources) and the technology that turns these factors of production into output. In the long run, the price level does not affect the production of output. In this time frame, the quantity of money determines the price level, according to the quantity theory.

Suppose a world with two economies. All else equal, the economy with more money in circulation will have a higher price level than the economy with less money in circulation. But the quantity

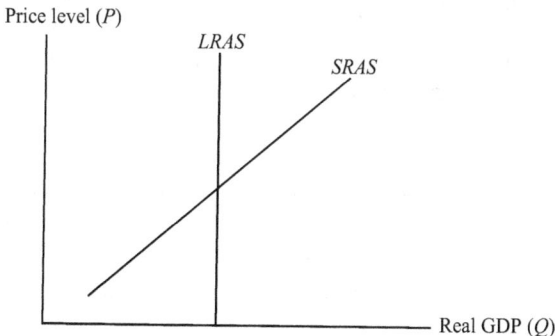

Figure 10.2 Long-run and short-run *AS* curves

of money does not impact technology or the supply of economic resources. As a result, the level of production in the two economies is identical.

Because the price level does not impact the long-run determinants of real GDP, *LRAS* is vertical. Regardless of the price level, the technology and quantity of capital, labor, and natural resources determine the level of output. The *LRAS* curve demonstrates the classical theory of money neutrality. To recall the theory, real variables do not depend on nominal variables. The *LRAS* curve demonstrates this reality: real GDP, a real variable, does not depend on the price level, a nominal variable.

Over longer periods of time, this principle provides a useful framework. But the principle does not explain short-run variations in economic activity. Two important questions exist.

First, what is the position of the *LRAS* curve? In the long run, the economy's level of production occurs at full-employment output or potential output. The reason is that, in the long run, the production of output occurs when unemployment is at its natural rate. Economists identify this point as the *natural level of output*, because the economy gravitates to it in the long run.

Second, when does the *LRAS* curve shift? The curve shifts when an economic change alters the natural level of output. The four sources of change are capital, labor, natural resources, and technology (Table 10.2). For example, an increase in labor force participation or immigration increases the quantity of labor. The result is a rightward shift in the *LRAS* curve. If an increase occurs in the stock of capital, level of labor, or availability of natural resources, or if technological advancement occurs, the *LRAS* curve increases, shifting rightward.

Table 10.2 Determinants of LRAS

Determinant	LRAS increases	LRAS decreases
Capital	Increases	Decreases
Labor	Increases	Decreases
Natural resources	Increase	Decrease
Technology	Increases	Decreases

The model of aggregate economic activity establishes a framework to describe long-run trends. Over longer periods of time, technological progress increases the ability of the economy to turn economic resource inputs into output. The result is a rightward shift in the *LRAS* curve. But at the same time the central bank increases the supply of money, shifting the *AD* curve rightward. The result is a long-term increase in both output and inflation, corresponding to the classical model.

SHORT-RUN AGGREGATE SUPPLY

While the *AD-AS* model describes long-term economic trends, the main purpose of the model is to analyze short-run economic activity. In the short run, deviations away from the natural rate of output serve as cyclical fluctuations, fueling business cycles. During the contractionary phase, the economy underperforms, with a rising rate of unemployment. During the expansionary phase, the economy grows, with a falling rate of unemployment.

In the short run, the shape of *SRAS* is important. In the short run, the price level affects the economy. In this time frame, an increase in the price level provides an incentive for firms to produce more goods and services. When the price level rises, the cost of some economic resources does not immediately change. For example, during an economic expansion, rents and wages may not initially change, because they are fixed. That is, these input prices are sticky. As a result, when output prices rise, profits increase, providing the incentive for firms to increase production. This is the reason that the *SRAS* curve slopes upward.

But sticky prices do not persist. When production increases, firms hire more workers or pay existing workers overtime. As the competition for employees increases, wages rise, leading to higher input costs. An increase in real GDP reduces the unemployment rate, creating a tighter labor market. In the short run, an increase in production along the *SRAS* curve leads to a higher price level.

In addition to the fact that the *SRAS* curve slopes upward, it may shift. All else equal, the determinants of *SRAS* include changes in inflationary expectations, the market power of firms, prices of economic resources, productivity, regulation, subsidies, and taxes (Table 10.3). For example, if business taxes fall, firms produce more output at a given price level, so the *SRAS* curve increases, shifting rightward. In general, an increase in *SRAS* occurs with a decrease in the prices of economic resources, lower inflationary expectations, a reduction in the market power of firms, higher levels of productivity, or a decrease in burdensome regulation.

MACROECONOMIC EQUILIBRIUM

The short-run macroeconomic equilibrium occurs at the intersection of *AD* and *SRAS*: point *a* in Figure 10.3. At equilibrium, price expectations are equal to $P^\star$. In the figure, point *a* represents a long-term macroeconomic equilibrium, because real GDP exists at the natural rate of output, that is, the full employment level of production (Q_f). At the equilibrium point, the unemployment rate is consistent with a low and consistent rate of inflation, equal to inflationary expectations. In macroeconomics, the model demonstrates why cyclical instability occurs: shifts in *AD* and/or *SRAS*, according to the determinants in Table 10.3, move the economy away from $P^\star$ and Q_f.

CYCLICAL INSTABILITY

The macroeconomic equilibrium in Figure 10.3 occurs at the full-employment level of production. This is a desired equilibrium. The reason is that the equilibrium point corresponds to Q_f. But this outcome may not persist. As Keynes explained, the economy may

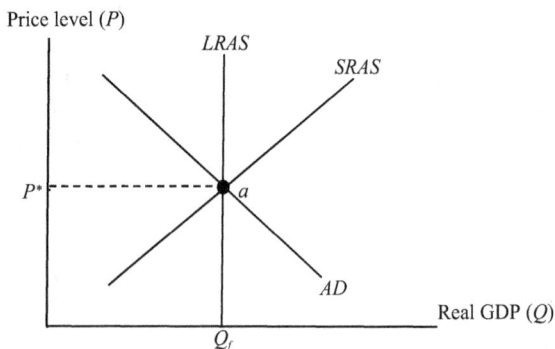

Figure 10.3 Macroeconomic equilibrium

Table 10.3 Determinants of SRAS

Determinant	SRAS *increases*	SRAS *decreases*
Inflationary expectations	Lower	Higher
Market power of firms	Lower	Higher
Prices of economic resources	Decrease	Increase
Productivity		
Human capital	Rises	Falls
Technology	Rises	Falls
Regulation		
Burdensome regulation	Decreases	Increases
Subsidies	Increase	Decrease
Taxes	Decrease	Increase

establish an equilibrium level of production at a point that differs from full employment, creating cyclical instability. In addition, the equilibrium may not lead to price-level stability. An undesired equilibrium means that *AD* intersects *SRAS* at a point different from Q_f and P^*. By analyzing economic activity during the Great Depression, Keynes argued that an undesired equilibrium could persist.

In this framework, Keynes asked, why should equilibrium occur at the optimal point? Many factors influence macroeconomic activity. The same factors may create an undesirable outcome. On the demand side, consumers, businesses, government, and foreign economic agents undertake independent spending decisions. They focus their spending behavior on current economic observations, expectations, and other factors. Because their spending decisions are independent, the sum of their expenditures may not correspond to the optimal amount of *AD*. In the Keynesian perspective, one of three outcomes may occur:

1   Optimal outcome: *AD* equals *SRAS* at Q_f and P^* (Figure 10.3)
2   Recessionary GDP gap: *AD* equals *SRAS*, when the equilibrium level of production $(Q_e) < Q_f$, and the equilibrium price level $(P_e) < P^*$ (Figure 10.4)
3   Inflationary GDP gap: *AD* equals *SRAS*, when $Q_e > Q_f$, and $P_e > P^*$ (Figure 10.5)

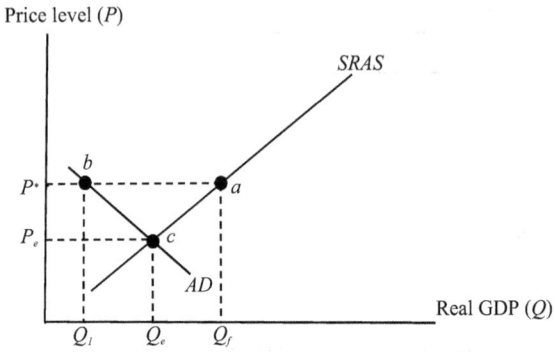

Figure 10.4 Recessionary GDP gap

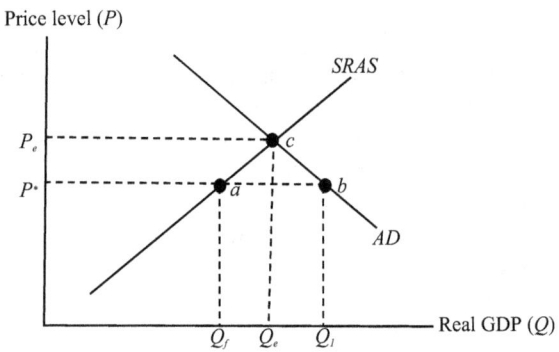

Figure 10.5 Inflationary GDP gap

RECESSIONARY GDP GAP

Figure 10.4 graphs the second outcome: a *recessionary GDP gap* ($Q_f - Q_e$), with an insufficient amount of *AD*. At point *a*, full-employment production exists at Q_f and a stable price level is at $P^\star$. But at $P^\star$ the level of aggregate output demanded falls short of Q_f. Why does this outcome occur? At $P^\star$, the spending by consumers, businesses, government, and foreign economic agents (point *b*) does not generate enough *AD* for the economy to operate at Q_f. This is an undesired outcome: at full employment, more output is produced than market participants want to buy. As the undesired inventory rises, production in the next period falls. Workers lose their jobs. The price level declines. The economy settles at point c, the undesired macroeconomic equilibrium.

For Keynes, the recessionary GDP gap was troubling because the actual level of real GDP fell short of the full-employment level of GDP. In his framework, the gap led to unused productive capacity, the contractionary phase of the business cycle, and cyclical unemployment. Keynes argued that if economic expectations were poor and business investment was low, the recessionary GDP gap could persist.

INFLATIONARY GDP GAP

Figure 10.5 graphs the third outcome: an *inflationary GDP gap* (Q_e − Q_f), with too much AD. At point a, full-employment production exists at Q_f, and a stable price level occurs at $P^\star$. But at $P^\star$, AD at point b exceeds the capacity of the economy to produce output along $SRAS$. In the figure, the AD curve includes spending from all economic agents in the economy. But at the stable price level ($P^\star$) and point b, the market participants demand a higher level of output (Q_1) than the market produces (Q_f). To meet the higher level of demand, firms hire more workers, use overtime, and increase their capacity to produce output. The result is an increase in the price level, a macroeconomic equilibrium at point c, and a higher price level (P_e). The undesirable equilibrium creates a context for demand-pull inflation.

Two goals of the macroeconomy are full-employment production and a stable price level. But in Keynes' general theory, undesirable outcomes may persist. According to Keynes, it is particularly troubling when an economy is stuck with a low level of production and a high rate of unemployment.

MACRO FAILURE

If the equilibrium level of real GDP differs from full employment, a macro failure exists. With a recessionary GDP gap, the unemployment rate is too high. With an inflationary GDP gap, the inflation rate is too high. Another outcome may result from supply-side changes: *stagflation*, when both the unemployment rate and inflation rates are too high. This possibility occurs after a supply shock, when the *SRAS* curve decreases, shifting leftward.

In the 1970s, stagflation resulted from a global oil shock. In many industries, an increase in energy prices led to a decrease in the production of output. A leftward shift in the *SRAS* curve from rising inflationary expectations led to a higher price level and less real GDP. The undesirable equilibrium created a context for cost-push inflation.

SELF-ADJUSTMENT OR INSTABILITY?

With cyclical instability, an important question relates to macro-economic equilibrium: if the economy experiences macro failure, will it self-adjust? That is, after a deviation away from the natural rate of output, will the economy gravitate back to Q_f? Two schools of thought, the classical school and Keynesian school, provide different answers.

According to classical economists, if consumer saving (a leak) is greater than business investment (an injection), households channel excess income into bank accounts. Banks are anxious to lend the money, and firms are willing to borrow. The interest rate falls, prompting the firms to borrow and invest. In classical economies, if the interest rate adjusts, investment will equal savings, returning the economy to Q_f.

Keynesianism provides a different answer. With this theory, if macro failure exists, an economy does not necessarily gravitate back to full employment. The economy could stagnate, experiencing a high unemployment rate. In this situation, a decrease in AD leads to excess inventories. In response, firms lay off employees, increasing the unemployment rate. A decrease in investment leads to a negative multiplier effect, reducing output and income. The economy contracts, without a return to full employment.

In the AD-AS model, if an economy is to return to full employment, a shortfall in AD must be offset by additional spending. For example, if household consumption falls, business investment must rise. But another scenario may occur. With negative economic sentiments, households and businesses may share a pessimistic forecast. But government policy may offset a decrease in consumption and investment. The government intervention may occur with a change in expenditure, taxation, or the money supply. These are the topics of Chapters 11 and 12. Before addressing these policies, however, consider three famous cases of macro failure: the Great Depression, Great Recession, and coronavirus pandemic.

THE GREAT DEPRESSION

The Great Depression of the 1930s, the longest and most severe economic downturn of the twentieth century, demonstrated that an economy could maintain a recessionary GDP gap. In the US, between 1929 and 1933, real GDP decreased by 26 percent. In the banking sector, financial friction increased the cost of intermediation, reducing the ability of firms to borrow money. A lag between the payments to labor inputs and revenue generation required financing. An inability to sell output and borrow money reduced the level of employment. The firms with the highest levels of debt fired workers. As a result, investment, the most volatile component of GDP, fell by nearly 80 percent. A decrease in consumption and investment from the layoffs and economic uncertainty reduced AD, leading to a decline in both output and income. The negative multiplier effect created an economic depression. An important variable was the unemployment rate. In 1932, the US unemployment rate peaked at 25 percent, the highest rate in the country's history. During the 1930s, the US unemployment rate never fell below 15 percent. Because the increase in AD that was necessary to restore the economy was so large, recovery did not occur until the 1940s, with government spending during World War II.

THE GREAT RECESSION

The Great Recession in the US, lasting from December 2007 to June 2009, followed a booming housing market. In the buildup to the crisis, many individuals bought houses for the purpose of speculation, not residential living. The period was characterized by rapidly rising housing prices, residential construction, and increasing consumer debt. Several factors triggered the growth in the housing sector, including low interest rates, market optimism, and relaxation of lending standards in the banking industry. Lightly-regulated financial institutions displaced some of the lending from traditional commercial banks, reducing the cost of mortgage financing. The result of the housing boom was an increase in the vulnerability of both households and banks. Households continued to borrow. Banks continued to lend. The market encouraged the behavior. By the end of 2007, housing prices began to decline. The ratio of household debt to annual income rose, signaling an inability of some households to pay back their loans. The downfall of household balance sheets established a pathway in which a fear of layoffs and a lower level of consumer spending impacted economic activity. In particular, the collapse of the housing bubble, decline in consumer confidence, and a decrease in investment led to a leftward shift in AD. Production fell below full employment. In the context of a contracting economy, the Great Recession resulted from a demand shock. The decrease in AD created a divergence between actual GDP and potential GDP, signaling a recessionary GDP gap. As firms fired workers, cyclical unemployment rose. During the recession, government policy was slow to solve the problem, prolonging the recovery.

THE CORONAVIRUS PANDEMIC

At the end of 2019, the disease COVID-19 began to spread throughout the world. From 2020–2020, the coronavirus pandemic led to widespread economic uncertainty. Economic contagion began in the developed world but spread throughout Asia, Africa, and South America. As a result of the pandemic shock, twin economic and health crises led to rising levels of morbidity, mortality, and unemployment, affecting billions of people. As exposure to the novel coronavirus rose, aggregate economic activity fell. Trying to put people back to work, countries experienced higher healthcare costs, medical shortages, and social anxiety. In response, governments implemented extensive forms of control, including household lockdowns and economic shutdowns. A leftward shift in $SRAS$ resulted from the decrease in production and a global supply chain disruption. The decrease in output on the supply side was exacerbated by a leftward shift in AD, resulting from rising unemployment, falling income, and a decrease in investment. Because the initial magnitude of the shift in *AD* exceeded the magnitude of the shift in *SRAS*, a decreasing price level accompanied the recessionary GDP gap. But the pandemic recession was short. The reason was that government stimulus plans supported both businesses and households. As consumption, investment, and government spending rose, *AD* increased, raising the price level. By the end of 2021, the inflation rate rose, causing central banks to decrease the money supply in economies around the world. Overall, the coronavirus pandemic created large-scale economic costs, the loss of millions of lives, and a long trail of disruption.

KEY TERMS

aggregate demand
aggregate supply
export price effect
inflationary GDP gap
interest rate effect
natural level of output
recessionary GDP gap
stagflation
wealth effect

FURTHER READING

Benmelech, Efraim, Frydman, Carola and Papanikolaou, Dimitris. 2019. "Financial Frictions and Employment During the Great Depression." *Journal of Financial Economics*, 133 (3): 541–563.

Gertler, Mark and Gilchrist, Simon. 2018. "What Happened: Financial Factors in the Great Recession." *Journal of Economic Perspectives*, 32 (3): 3–30.

Guerrieri, Veronica, Lorenzoni, Guido, Straub, Ludwig and Werning, Iván. 2022. "Macroeconomic Implications of COVID-19: Can Negative Supply Shocks Cause Demand Shortages?" *American Economic Review*, 112 (5): 1437–1474.

PART V
STABILIZATION POLICY

FISCAL POLICY

FISCAL RESPONSE TO THE GREAT RECESSION

The Great Recession (2007–2009), which began in the United States (US), spread to the European Union (EU). The downturn increased the unemployment rate and decreased household income. On a global scale, the crisis reduced world trade, exacerbating the economic problems. But in the EU, the recession triggered a large-scale fiscal response. Activist government policy addressed the crisis. The fiscal policies enacted in the EU, including government borrowing and spending, enhanced economic activity and reduced the severity of the crisis.

This chapter argues that governments use policy to smooth cyclical fluctuations. When the economy is slumping, injections into the income stream stimulate production, increase income, and reduce unemployment. Because government intervention alters economic activity, the chapter discusses stabilization policies, fiscal policy and aggregate demand, fiscal policy and aggregate supply, the multiplier effects of fiscal policy, budget deficits and government debt, and the shortcomings of fiscal policy. By reading the chapter, students will understand the potential for public policy to counter cyclical fluctuations.

STABILIZATION POLICIES

Downturns in economic activity do not last forever. In the United Kingdom (UK) and US, recessions often last less than a year. The Great Recession was an exception. Why are most recessions brief?

DOI: 10.4324/9781003678700-16

Two reasons exist. First, government intervention limits economic contraction. Second, when production declines, the economy has the ability to self-correct.

During an economic contraction, governments may boost production, reduce unemployment, and reverse the recessionary trend. One method is to increase aggregate demand (*AD*). Another method is to increase long-run aggregate supply (*LRAS*). For an economic recovery, actual production must increase to full-employment output.

To alter economic activity, governments implement *fiscal policy* (the topic of this chapter), which is the use of government expenditure (spending) and revenue collection (taxation) to alter economic activity. Alternatively, central banks implement monetary policy (the topic of the next chapter), which alters the money supply, credit, and interest rates.

Fiscal policy includes both spending and revenue components. Governments implement *expansionary fiscal policy* to fight recessions, and *contractionary fiscal policy* to fight inflation. While the former stimulates economic activity, the latter slows the rate of economic growth. What are the tools of expansionary fiscal policy? The answer is an increase in government expenditure (*G*), a decrease in taxation (*T*), or an increase in transfer payments (*TR*). The latter are the payments to groups or individuals, when no service is required in return. For contractionary fiscal policy, governments reduce *G*, raise *T*, or decrease *TR*.

G AS A COMPONENT OF FISCAL POLICY

Government spending includes the purchase of goods and services, such as roads, bridges, highways, education, military expenditures, and wages for government workers. The expenditure exists within the annual government budget and the spending component of GDP. The government budget also includes *TR*. With the latter, the government transfers money from one group to another. Examples include food, health, and income assistance. In general, *government outlays* include both spending and *TR*. But three types of outlays exist: discretionary spending, mandatory outlays, and interest payments.

Discretionary spending is approved and allocated on an annual basis. Policy makers alter discretionary spending according to budgetary circumstances. For example, when the economy is growing and tax revenue is increasing, governments build more roads, bridges, and highways.

Mandatory spending is required by law, differing from discretionary spending. Mandatory spending includes entitlement programs, such as payments to retirees or healthcare benefits to low-income households.

Interest payments flow to holders of government debt. If the government borrows money, it must pay back the principal plus interest. The interest payments are a different form of mandatory expenditures.

Over time, G responds to changes in economic circumstances. Economists view an increase in G as a response to a rising rate of unemployment. But they view an increase in T as a response to a rising rate of inflation. From a policy perspective, changes in G and T modify cyclical fluctuations.

T AS A COMPONENT OF FISCAL POLICY

Government expenditures require the reallocation of money from the private sector to the public sector. To finance government programs, economic agents surrender their right to use some of their monetary resources. Governments implement T, which are compulsory payments for specific economic activities, to generate revenue and/or alter economic activity.

The method of financing impacts the efficiency with which resources are used, the prices of goods and services, and the distribution of income. While income taxes fund federal and state governments, property taxes fund local governments. But taxes on imports discourage the purchase of foreign goods and services, providing the incentive for the consumption of domestically-produced output. The problem is that the revenue generated from T may not correspond to the monetary requirements of G.

With fiscal policy, a decrease in T leads to an increase in disposable income and spending, a rightward shift in AD, and an expansionary impact. In contrast, an increase in T leads to a decrease in disposable income and spending, a leftward shift in AD, and a contractionary impact.

TR AS A COMPONENT OF FISCAL POLICY

Transfers redistribute purchasing power. For low-income households, retirees, and the unemployed, they serve as income support. But the recipients are not required to undertake any services in return. In contrast, the recipients meet a specific qualification, such as an income level, age, or unemployment status. Transfer programs to assist low-income households consist of direct cash transfers, direct provision of goods and services (such as medical care), and subsidies for food and housing. While economists debate the extent to which transfers alter the behavior of the recipients, the magnitude of the programs highlights their importance. In many countries, including the UK and US, transfers are a significant portion of the government budget. With respect to fiscal policy, an increase in TR has an expansionary outcome. A decrease in TR has a contractionary outcome. The extent that a change in TR alters economic activity depends on the specific form of policy, magnitude of the payment, and time frame.

AUTOMATIC STABILIZERS

Fiscal policy involves the executive and legislative branches of government. Policy complexities complicate the process, including form, size, and timing. But a certain level of macroeconomic stability exists. For example, transfers and tax revenue exist as *automatic stabilizers*. These variables change in ways that counter the business cycle. When the economy expands, tax revenue rises. At the same time, transfers fall, because fewer individuals require public assistance. When the economy slumps, tax revenue declines, but transfers rise, cushioning the impact of the downturn. While transfers and tax revenue do not eliminate cyclical fluctuations, the variables decrease their intensity.

FISCAL POLICY AND AGGREGATE DEMAND

When the economy slips into a recession, the government may reverse the trend. In addition, if the economy experiences inflation, the government may intervene. In both cases, policy tools exist. To shift AD, policymakers alter G, T, or TR. In most countries, these changes are legislated.

EXPANSIONARY FISCAL POLICY AND *AD*

Increases in *G*, decrease in *T*, or higher level of *TR* are expansionary, shifting the *AD* curve rightward (Figure 11.1). When AD_0 shifts to AD_1, both real GDP and the price level rise, boosting the economy from equilibrium output (Q_e) to full-employment output (Q_f).

Because full employment is a macroeconomic goal, the stabilization policy reduces cyclical instability, reversing the contraction. But the outcome includes a less-desirable outcome: a higher rate of inflation. Expansionary fiscal policy takes one of three forms:

- Increase in *G*
- Decrease in *T*
- Increase in *TR*

CONTRACTIONARY FISCAL POLICY AND *AD*

When the economy moves beyond full-employment output, the inflation rate increases. In response, a reduction in *G*, increase in *T*, or decrease in *TR* shifts AD_0 leftward to AD_1, reducing both real GDP from Q_e to Q_f and the rate of inflation from P_e to $P^\star$ (Figure 11.2).

Demand-side policies create a tradeoff between output and the price level. When the inflation rate is rising, the fiscal policy that

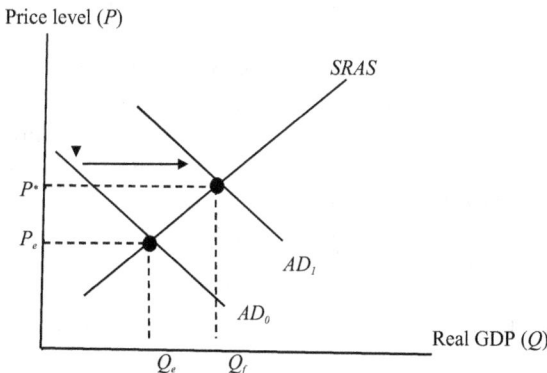

Figure 11.1 Expansionary fiscal policy and an increase in *AD*

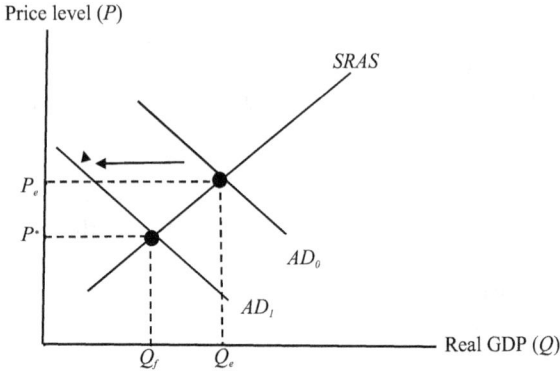

Figure 11.2 Contractionary fiscal policy and a decrease in *AD*

reverses the trend leads to an increase in the unemployment rate. Contractionary fiscal policy takes one of three forms:

- Decrease in G
- Increase T
- Decrease in TR

FISCAL POLICY AND AGGREGATE SUPPLY

In addition to *AD*, fiscal policy may alter *LRAS*. Supply-side policy focuses on long-run economic growth. What fiscal policies generate an increase in full-employment output? First, spending on infrastructure, including a country's roads, bridges, highways, and communication systems, increases the economy's productive capacity. Over longer time periods, the spending creates jobs, improves efficiency, and reduces costs. Second, a decrease in business taxes reduces the cost of production, increasing profitability. The policy provides the incentive for firms to increase supply. Third, an increase in investment from productivity gains increases *LRAS*. Policies such as investment tax credits, more rapid depreciation schedules, and grants for basic research, result in new products and technology. Fourth, repealing unnecessary business regulations reduces costs and provides an incentive for building and product development.

These policies do not involve a tradeoff between output and the price level. But supply-side policies take time to unfold. The rightward shift in the $LRAS$ curve increases both full-employment output from Q_{f0} to Q_{f1} and the economy's productive capacity (Figure 11.3). At the peak of the next business cycle, the economy employs more workers. When $LRAS$ shifts to the right, lower prices for economic resources lead to an increase in production. As a result, the $SRAS_0$ curve shifts rightward to $SRAS_1$.

MULTIPLIER EFFECTS

In the above discussion, fiscal policy shifts AD or $LRAS$. In addition to the direction of the shift, economists use the multiplier effect to forecast how much of a shift will occur.

THE MULTIPLIER EFFECT OF A CHANGE IN G

The first fiscal policy option is a change in G. In response to the coronavirus pandemic, spending by the government of the UK was £179 billion higher during 2020–2021 than it would have been in the absence of the pandemic. The public spending supported firms, individuals, and public services, such as healthcare and social care. Even though the pandemic shocked the economy, the government intervention helped the economy reverse course.

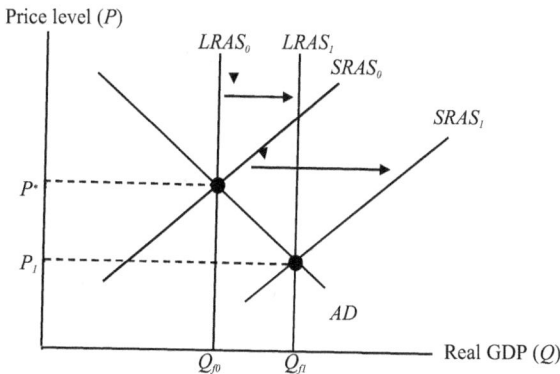

Figure 11.3 Expansionary fiscal policy and $LRAS$

The policy increased total spending by £179 billion. But what was the multiplier effect? To answer the question, it is important to acknowledge that, throughout the economy, government policy started a chain reaction. The increase in income led to a rise in consumer spending. The rise in consumer spending provided an incentive for firms to produce more output, which led to a further increase in income, and so forth.

In general, the overall impact of fiscal policy depends on the multiplier effect. From a policy perspective, the multiplier equals the ratio of the change in real GDP ($/Delta Y$) to the initial fiscal stimulus, such as the change in spending from government policy ($/Delta G$):

$$multiplier = \frac{\Delta \, real \, GDP}{Initial \, fiscal \, stimulus} = \frac{\Delta Y}{\Delta G}$$

Suppose three simplifying assumptions. First, changes to real GDP accrue to households. Second, the price level is fixed, so a change in nominal GDP is also a change in real GDP. Third, the interest rate is fixed, so the cost of borrowing remains constant. These assumptions maximize the multiplier effect.

In the framework, economists calculate the numerical value of the multiplier as $1/(1 - MPC)$, where the MPC is the marginal propensity to consume. If the $MPC = 0.80$, the multiplier $= 1/(1- 0.80) = 1/0.20 = 5$. Given this value, the increase in government spending results in an overall impact of:

$$\Delta Y = (multiplier) \, (Initial \, fiscal \, stimulus)$$

$$= (5) \, (£ \, 79 \, billion) = £ \, 895 \, billion$$

Of the £895 billion overall impact, £179 billion is the initial effect of the increase in G and £716 billion is the secondary impact. The overall effect depends on the MPC. If the MPC is higher, the multiplier effect rises. If the MPC is lower, the multiplier effect falls.

THE MULTIPLIER EFFECT OF A CHANGE IN T

The second fiscal policy option is a change in T. Compared to a change in G, a change in T modifies income in a different way.

Taxes are payments from economic agents to the government. Tax bases include income, property, and sales. How does a change in T impact the economy? To answer the question, remember that, in macroeconomic equilibrium, injections into the economy equal leakages out of the economy:

$$I + G + X = S + T + M,$$

where investment (I), government expenditure, and exports (X) are the injections and savings (S), taxes, and imports (M) are the leakages. A decrease in T creates two outcomes. First, the policy increases the disposable income of consumers. Second, equilibrium income rises. But consumers will not spend the entire tax cut. They will save some of the money. The key is the MPC. If the $MPC = 0.80$, consumers in the UK spend £0.80 out of every tax cut of £1.00:

$$Initial\, fiscal\, stimulus\, =\, (MPC)\, (Tax\, cut)$$

With respect to the previous change in G, consider the equivalent decrease in T. If T decreases by £179 billion, the initial change in consumption is:

$$Initial\, fiscal\, stimulus\, =\, (0.80)\, (£179\, billion)\, =\, £\, 143.2\, billion$$

In this case, the tax cut increases disposable income, stimulates consumer spending, and shifts AD to the right. But the overall change in income equals the multiplier times the initial change in consumption:

$$\Delta Y\, =\, (multiplier)\, (Initial\, fiscal\, stimulus)$$
$$=\, (5)\, (£143.2\, billion)\, =\, £\, 716\, billion$$

The result is that a change in T impacts the economy less than the equivalent change in G. The reason is that, compared to the implementation of a change in G, the decrease in T has less fiscal stimulus. When T decreases, consumers save some of the money.

Thus, the size of the tax cut is greater than the initial injection in spending. Government purchases stimulate the economy more than an equivalent amount of tax cuts.

THE MULTIPLIER EFFECT OF A CHANGE IN *TR*

The third fiscal policy option is a change in *TR*. If the government transfers more money to individuals for food, healthcare, social security, or unemployment benefits, disposable income rises. The resulting increase in consumption leads to a rightward shift in *AD*. But more transfers do not increase injections on an equivalent basis. As with a decrease in *T*, individuals save some of the additional transfers. The policy injects a portion of the additional income, according to the *MPC*, into the economy's spending:

$$Initial\,fiscal\,stimulus\, =\, (MPC)\,(\Delta TR)$$

The change in *TR* initiates the multiplier effect, shifting the *AD* curve.

BUDGET DEFICITS AND GOVERNMENT DEBT

Fiscal policy is useful to address two macroeconomic problems: inflation and unemployment. If the inflation rate is rising, contractionary fiscal policy slows economic activity, decreases income, and reduces the price level. If the unemployment rate is rising, expansionary fiscal policy stimulates economic activity, increases income, and creates jobs. But the use of the government budget to alter economic activity means that government expenditures and receipts will not always equalize. The government may experience a budget deficit:

$$Budget\,deficit\, =\, G\, -\, T\, >\, 0$$

The government may also experience a budget surplus:

$$Budget\,surplus\, =\, G\, -\, T\, <\, 0$$

To demonstrate the outcome of fiscal policy, economists identify two parts of the budget balance:

$$Budget\,balance\,=\,cyclical\,balance\,+\,structural\,balance$$

CYCLICAL BALANCE

The existence of deficits or surpluses links to the economy. With economic growth, both income and output rise, increasing employment. In this case, the increase in economic activity leads to more tax payments flowing to the government, reducing budget deficits or raising budget surpluses. In addition, during expansionary times, there is no need for an increase in G. But with economic contraction, both income and output fall, decreasing employment. In this case, the decrease in economic activity leads to less tax payments flowing to the government, raising budget deficits or reducing budget surpluses. During contractionary times, there is a need for an increase in G, contributing to the budgetary outcome.

The point is that policymakers do not have complete control over the budget. Both economic conditions and government policy impact budgetary outcomes. With a deficit, the part of the government budget attributable to cyclical fluctuations in employment and inflation is a *cyclical deficit*. In this context, when the rate of economic growth increases or the rate of inflation decreases, the cyclical deficit falls. But when the rate of economic growth decreases or the rate of inflation increases, the cyclical deficit rises. In other words, the cyclical balance reflects the impact of the business cycle on both government spending and tax revenue.

STRUCTURAL BALANCE

The structural part of the government balance reflects policy decisions. As opposed to comparing actual government spending to actual receipts, economists analyze the budget balance that would exist at full employment. The *structural deficit* is a measure of full-employment outlays versus receipts, eliminating the portion of the budget balance from cyclical fluctuations. In this context, part of the budget balance stems from cyclical economic conditions;

however, the remaining portion stems from fiscal policy, the structural balance.

With the two parts of the budget balance, economists assign responsibility for a rising budget deficit. That is, economists acknowledge that both automatic stabilizers and fiscal policies impact the budget balance. To identify the impact of fiscal policy, economists focus on changes in the structural deficit, not the overall deficit. In particular, expansionary fiscal policy leads to an increase in the structural deficit or a decrease in the structural surplus. But contractionary fiscal policy leads to a decrease in the structural deficit or an increase in the structural surplus.

THE ACCUMULATION OF GOVERNMENT DEBT

Annual budget deficits lead to the accumulation of government debt. By issuing debt instruments, such as bills, notes, and bonds, governments finance deficits. By issuing debt instruments, however, governments must repay the lenders. The holders of government debt include government agencies, the central bank, individuals in the private sector, foreign economic agents, and state and local governments.

Debt instruments are assets for the economic agents who purchase them, but liabilities for the governments who repay them. That is, the holders of the debt instruments have a claim to future payments. They may hold the instruments until maturity or sell them in financial markets. As the government debt rises, the level of wealth to economic agents increases by the same amount.

The burden of debt includes annual interest payments, the cost of refinancing, the opportunity cost of the activities financed by the debt, and the resulting trade-offs. Economists calculate the *debt-to-GDP ratio* as a measure of a country's national debt to its annual output. When the variable exceeds one hundred percent, economists are concerned that the government debt will create an undue burden.

SHORTCOMINGS OF FISCAL POLICY

In practice, the effect of fiscal policy depends on the link between the policy and economic circumstances. If the policy is too timid, it may not achieve the desired result. If it is too aggressive, it may lead to undesired consequences, such as an increase in the inflation rate. While fiscal policy may reverse an economic contraction, it does not always work as planned. If economic outcomes stem from changes in G, T, TR, and the multiplier process, why do the contractionary phases of the business cycle occur? In general, fiscal policy impacts millions of firms and individuals. After policy implementation, the collective decisions of economic agents affect the economy. How much fiscal policy is enough to alter economic activity? A priori, economists do not necessarily know the specific answer. As a result, policymakers have to take an adaptive approach. Five claims raise specific concerns about fiscal policy.

CLAIM 1: BUDGET DEFICITS REDUCE PRIVATE SPENDING

As this chapter explains, expansionary fiscal policy increases budget deficits and government debt. To pay for the debt, the tax revenue flowing to the government must rise, either through higher tax receipts from the growing economy, higher tax rates, or both. This claim implies that economic agents forecast higher future taxes, so they increase their savings today. Thus, current consumption declines. This outcome, known as *Ricardian equivalence*, after the economist David Ricardo (1772–1823), means that financing through government debt leads to an adjustment of consumer spending, without a shift in *AD*. Individuals respond to the government policy with an increase in savings. Although the claim is possible, what is the problem? In reality, economic agents may not respond with foresight and discipline. When individuals have more money, they spend it, according to the *MPC*. Therefore, expansionary fiscal policy creates the conditions for economic growth.

CLAIM 2: FISCAL POLICY CROWDS OUT PRIVATE INVESTMENT

Crowding out means that a higher level of government spending reduces private-sector spending. The idea is that government borrowing (and subsequent spending) takes funds out of the economy that would have been used for private investment. How valid is the claim? It is true that a higher level of government borrowing increases the demand for loanable funds, raising the interest rate. But the outcome depends on the state of the economy. If the economy experiences a strong level of economic growth and firms are operating at capacity, a higher interest rate may crowd out private investment. But if the economy is operating in the contractionary phase of the business cycle, operating at less than full employment, expansionary fiscal policy raises aggregate income. At any interest rate, the increase in income will raise both consumption and savings. The larger pool of savings means the government may borrow more money without raising interest rates. Many examples of this outcome exist, such as the US government response to the Great Recession, when the fiscal expansion did not lead to higher interest rates.

CLAIM 3: FISCAL POLICY HAS A TIME LAG

For many economists, the evaluation of fiscal policy means that governments should maintain an active stabilization policy. While fiscal policy does not solve all macroeconomic problems, it often is effective in addressing cyclical instability. But some economists argue that an active fiscal policy itself may lead to instability. An important reason is the existence of a *time lag*, the delay between policy implementation and the outcome. The time lag may be significant. To evaluate the problem, consider the sequence of events for expansionary fiscal policy:

• The government identifies a recessionary GDP gap by collecting and analyzing data
• The government formulates a policy response with a spending plan
• With the spending plan, the executive and legislative branches pass the plan
• After the plan passes, the government increases G, decreases T, or raises TR

Each step takes time. Because of the time lag, the economy may recover before the full multiplier effect. In addition, the policy may lead to inflation. The latter outcome requires additional policy. The claim that fiscal policy has a time lag is true. But it does not mean that governments should avoid fiscal policy. In reality, the impact of fiscal policy on AD is often appropriate. But the existence of the time lag complicates the process.

CLAIM 4: FISCAL POLICY LEADS TO A BIAS TOWARD BORROWING AND AWAY FROM TAXATION

Because fiscal policy requires government intervention, the political process looms as a policy variable. A political bias may exist. That is, policymakers may prioritize borrowing instead of taxing. The choice may be a political reality, without an economic justification. One reason is that borrowing occurs through the issuance of debt instruments, making it more politically feasible. Another reason is that borrowing encourages the public sector to spread the cost of spending over a longer period of time, rather than incurring the cost at once through a change in the tax code. The consequence of more borrowing, however, is an increase in the annual deficit, government debt, interest payments, and the potential for crowding out.

CLAIM 5: FISCAL POLICY MAY NOT CONSIDER A SHIFT IN SAVINGS

The impact of an increase in G depends on how much households spend and save. Suppose the government of the UK sends households £1,000 each. If the $MPC = 0.80$, the multiplier equals 5. If the overall size of the government spending equals £1 billion, the change in output is:

$$\Delta Y = (multiplier)(\Delta G) = (5)(£1\ billion) = £5\ billion$$

But if the actual MPC is lower than the estimate, households save more. The result is that fiscal policy will not impact the economy as much. If the $MPC = 0.50$, the multiplier equals 2, and the policy effect is weaker:

$$\Delta Y = (multiplier)(\Delta G) = (2)(£1\ billion) = £2\ billion$$

Of course, the MPC could be higher, leading to a larger multiplier effect.

KEY TERMS

automatic stabilizers
contractionary fiscal policy

crowding out
cyclical deficit
debt-to-GDP ratio
expansionary fiscal policy
fiscal policy
government outlays
Ricardian equivalence
structural deficit
time lag

FURTHER READING

Coenen, Günter, Straub, Roland and Trabandt, Mathias. 2012. "Fiscal Policy and the Great Recession in the Euro Area." *American Economic Review*, 102 (3), 71–76.

Hausman, Joshua. 2016. "Fiscal Policy and Economic Recovery: The Case of the 1936 Veterans' Bonus." *American Economic Review*, 106 (4): 1100–1143.

Romer, Christina. 2021. "The Fiscal Policy Response to the Pandemic." *Brookings Papers on Economic Activity*, 1970 (1): 89–110.

MONETARY POLICY

MONETARY POLICY IN ACTION

During the 1980s and 1990s, many central banks—the financial institutions that oversee the money supplies of economies—had to fight inflation. But timely policy implementation, including higher interest rates, succeeded in solving the problem. The outcome brought economic stability into the new century.

In many countries, the first two decades of the century were associated with a low and steady rate of inflation, a sign of economic stability. The stability put central banks in a position to fight short-run fluctuations in output and income without having to worry about a rising price level. But low inflation became associated with low real interest rates.

The latter resulted from demographic, economic, and technological shifts that increased global savings relative to investment. The problem was that persistently low interest rates became a problem for central banks. Central banks may increase or decrease the money supply and alter interest rates, according to economic conditions. But when real interest rates are low, traditional forms of monetary policy do not have the same flexibility. To stimulate the economy, central banks often choose to increase the money supply, lower interest rates, and encourage borrowing and investment. But if interest rates are low, central banks are constrained.

As a result, central banks developed new policy tools, including forward guidance and quantitative easing. The former is a communication tool in which the central bank informs the public about likely future paths of interest rates. The latter is a tool

DOI: 10.4324/9781003678700-17

whereby the central bank purchases assets and injects liquidity into the economy. Both of the tools proved to be effective, demonstrating that central banks are flexible in responding to changing economic conditions.

To demonstrate this point, the chapter discusses the meaning of monetary policy, tools of monetary policy, monetary policy and aggregate demand, monetary policy and economic shocks, interest rate targets, the Eurozone and European central bank, and the Federal Reserve System.

WHAT IS MONETARY POLICY?

The study of macroeconomics demonstrates that the business cycle leads to changes in the production of output and the price level. During this century, the Great Recession (2007–2009) and coronavirus pandemic (2020–2022) serve as examples of economic downturns. When the economy slumps, the unemployment rate rises. The study of macroeconomics entails the analysis of cyclical fluctuations and how to address them. One way is through fiscal policy, the subject of the previous chapter. The other is monetary policy, the subject of this chapter.

The central bank controls monetary policy, which means adjusting the economy's money supply, interest rates, and availability of credit. The twin goals of central banks are a low and stable price level and low unemployment. Of course, these goals may come in conflict, especially during an economic expansion. In response, the central bank may choose one goal over the other. In this situation, it normally prioritizes a low and stable inflation rate.

Two types of monetary policy exist. When the economy is growing but the rate of inflation is rising, the central bank may implement a *contractionary monetary policy* that slows the economy and reduces the rate of inflation. This policy reduces the money supply, raises interest rates, and decreases the availability of credit. Alternatively, when the economy is slumping, the central bank may implement an *expansionary monetary policy* that stimulates the economy and reduces the unemployment rate. This policy raises the money supply, reduces interest rates, and increases the availability of credit.

TOOLS OF MONETARY POLICY

The central banks has three tools of monetary policy:

- Reserve requirement
- Discount rate
- Open market operations

RESERVE REQUIREMENT

As the chapter on money and banking explains, commercial banks are required by law to keep a certain amount of reserves on hand, according to the required reserve ratio (RRR). The reserves are held as either vault cash or deposits in the banks' reserve accounts with the central bank. As a first tool of monetary policy, the central bank may alter the RRR, adjusting the lending capacity of the banking system.

The ability of the banking system to create deposits and loan money is a function of the level of excess reserves held by banks and the money multiplier. The central bank impacts both of these variables through the RRR. For example, suppose banks collectively hold $200 billion in deposits and $50 billion in reserves. If the RRR = 10 percent, the banks are holding more reserves than they are required to hold:

$$Required\,reserves = (RRR)\,(deposits)$$

$$= (0.10)\,(\$200\,billion) = \$20\,billion$$

Because the banks are holding $50 billion in reserves, excess reserves exist:

$$Excess\,reserves = reserves - required\,reserves =$$
$$\$50\,billion - \$20\,billion = \$30\,billion$$

The excess reserves mean that the banking system has the power to lend. With the $30 billion in excess reserves and the money multiplier, the banking system may create deposits. In this case, the money multiplier is:

$$Money\,multiplier = \frac{1}{RRR} = \frac{1}{0.10} = 10$$

The potential for additional loans in the banking system is:

Deposit creating potential of the banking system

$$= (money\,multiplier)\,(excess\,reserves)$$

$$= (10)\,(\$30\,billion) = \$300\,billion$$

Without any additional reserves, the banking system could create another \$300 billion in transaction account balances (new money).

But what if the central bank wants to alter the lending capacity of the banking system? By changing the RRR, the central bank implements expansionary monetary policy (with a lower RRR) or contractionary monetary policy (with a higher RRR). Consider each case.

Suppose a slumping economy and a rising unemployment rate. The central bank may enact expansionary policy by reducing the RRR to 5 percent and increasing the money multiplier to 20. In this case, the lending capacity of the banking system rises, stimulating economic activity, encouraging businesses to borrow for capital investment, increasing aggregate demand (*AD*), and reducing the unemployment rate:

Deposit creating potential of the banking system

$$= (money\,multiplier)\,(excess\,reserves)$$

$$= (20)\,(\$30\,billion) = \$600\,billion$$

But a rising rate of inflation encourages the central bank to enact contractionary policy by raising the RRR to 20 percent and decreasing the money multiplier to 5. In this case, the lending capacity of the banking system falls, reducing economic activity, lowering capital investment, decreasing *AD*, and reducing the inflation rate:

Deposit creating potential of the banking system

$$= (money\ multiplier)\,(excess\ reserves)$$

$$= (5)\,(\$30\ billion) = \$150\ billion$$

By adjusting the RRR, the central bank alters the excess reserves, money multiplier, and lending capacity of the banking system. Although a change in the required reserves serves as a tool of monetary policy, the central bank of the United States (US) rarely alters it. The reason is the disruption to the banking system and credit markets. Even small changes to the RRR may have destabilizing effects. Similarly, the central bank of the European Union rarely alters the RRR.

DISCOUNT RATE

In addition to a change in the reserve requirement, the central bank may alter the *discount rate*, the second tool of monetary policy. The discount rate is the rate the central bank charges commercial banks for short-term borrowing. For commercial banks, the discount window of the central bank serves as a backup source of liquidity to meet reserve requirements.

Changes in the discount rate alter the cost of borrowing. If the central bank wants to implement expansionary monetary policy, it lowers the discount rate. If it wants to implement contractionary monetary policy, it raises the discount rate.

As an option, commercial banks may borrow from other banks in the federal funds market, if they are short on reserves. But they may also borrow from the central bank. To facilitate overnight borrowing, the central bank uses discount rate credit. The discount rate is normally higher than the federal funds rate to encourage commercial banks to borrow from each other, using the central bank as a last resort.

Typically, commercial banks avoid borrowing from the central bank's discount window. They do not want to raise concerns among depositors and the central bank about liquidity problems. But the central bank is willing to extend discount credit to make sure banks do not risk bankruptcy. Overall, the reserve requirement and discount rate are tools of monetary policy, but they do not have the power of the third tool of monetary policy.

OPEN MARKET OPERATIONS

The third and most important tool of monetary policy occurs when the central bank undertakes an *open market operation* (OMO) by buying or selling government securities in the open market. The tool offers the central bank a large degree of control and flexibility in altering both the money supply and interest rates. As a result, OMOs exist as the primary tool of monetary policy.

To evaluate the impact of OMOs, consider the portfolio choice of economic agents. They must decide how to use idle funds, such as money in bank accounts. Economic agents may keep idle funds in the bank. But they may also purchase stocks, bonds, or mutual funds.

The portfolio choice depends on risk, liquidity, and return. Bank account balances are highly liquid and do not experience market risk, but they have zero or low rates of return. Stocks, bonds, and mutual funds, however, entail higher rates of return with dividends, interest, and capital appreciation. (Stocks, bonds, and mutual funds differ with respect to their degrees of risk and liquidity.) The portfolio decision is the choice of where to keep idle funds. A balanced portfolio entails a mix of financial assets that have different degrees of risk, liquidity, and return.

With an OMO, the central bank buys or sells government securities. If the central bank buys securities in an expansionary form of monetary policy:

- Bank reserves rise
- The money supply increases
- Interest rates decrease
- The policy stimulates the economy

If the central bank sells securities in a contractionary form of monetary policy:

- Bank reserves fall
- The money supply decreases

- Interest rates increase
- The policy slows the economy

The central bank's actions therefore focus on the portfolio choice of economic agents. On the one hand, economic agents may hold idle funds in bank accounts. On the other hand, they may purchase securities, such as government bonds. As economic circumstances warrant, the central bank makes bonds more or less attractive. The objective of the central bank is to either encourage economic agents to move money from the bond market to banks or vice versa. Along the way, reserves in the banking system rise or fall, influencing the lending capacity of the banking system.

The two categories of monetary policy lead to different outcomes. When the central bank enacts expansionary monetary policy, it purchases bonds in the open market, increasing reserves and the deposit-creating potential of the banking system. When the central bank enacts contractionary monetary policy, it sells bonds in the open market, decreasing reserves and the deposit-creating potential of the banking system. The former is to increase employment. The latter is to decrease the rate of inflation.

To consider OMOs in more detail, consider the bond market. Not all economic agents purchase bonds, but many do. The central bank exists as a major institution in the bond market. What are the characteristics of the market? First, the bond market exists as a mechanism to channel money from lenders to borrowers. In the market, a corporation or government agency issues bonds, which are securities that offer proof of the promise to repay the loan. Because the corporations or government agencies are well known to the public, the bonds are actively traded in the bond market. Second, the owner of a bond does not have to wait until the bond reaches its maturity. The owner may sell the bond at any time at a price that is determined in the market.

The reason to purchase a bond is to earn interest. During the length of time to maturity, such as 10 years, the borrower must pay interest to the owner of the bond. For a $1,000 bond, with a 10-year period of time to maturity, issued at 5 percent interest, the issuing agency must pay $50 interest annually. At the end of the period, the issuing agency repays the initial $1,000. The *yield*, which is the rate of return on the bond, depends on the purchase price and interest rate:

$$Yield = \frac{annual\,interest\,payment}{bond\,price}$$

With a $1,000 price, the current yield is:

$$Yield = \frac{\$50}{\$1,000} = 0.05,\ or\ 5\ percent$$

But the bond market may set a different price than the face value. The demand for or supply of bonds may alter the price. For example, if the price increases to $1,050, the yield decreases:

$$Yield = \frac{\$50}{\$1,050} = 0.048,\ or\ 4.8\ percent$$

It is important to note that bond prices and yields move in the opposite direction. Although the bond market may alter the current price, the objective of the central bank, when issuing OMOs, is to influence both the price of bonds and their yields.

With expansionary policy and open market purchases, the central bank establishes bonds as a less attractive option for idle funds. In particular, the central bank offers to pay a higher price, reducing the yield. How do economic agents respond? They increase the deposits in their bank accounts. With an open market purchase, the central bank increases the money supply by increasing the reserves in the banking system. With an open market sale and contractionary policy, the central bank decreases the money supply by decreasing the reserves in the banking system.

POLICY OPTIONS

In sum, to increase the money supply with expansionary policy, the central bank may:

- Decrease the reserve requirement
- Reduce the discount rate
- Buy bonds with open market operations

To decrease the money supply with contractionary policy, the central bank may:

- Increase the reserve requirement
- Raise the discount rate
- Sell bonds with open market operations

MONETARY POLICY AND AGGREGATE DEMAND

The discussion in this book on the downward-sloping AD curve demonstrates that, for any given price level, AD shifts when the quantity of output changes. An important variable that shifts the AD curve is monetary policy. To illustrate the process in the short run, suppose the central bank purchases government bonds in the open market. The idea is to pump money into the banking system, increase the money supply (MS), and stimulate economic activity. How does the policy impact the equilibrium interest rate? To answer the question and reveal how monetary policy impacts AD, consider the structure of the money market.

In Figure 12.1, the downward-sloping money demand curve (MD) intersects the vertical money supply curve (MS_0) at the equilibrium interest rate (r_0). Because the central bank controls the money supply, MS_0 is vertical. When MS_0 shifts rightward to MS_1 with expansionary policy, the interest rate decreases to r_1. The

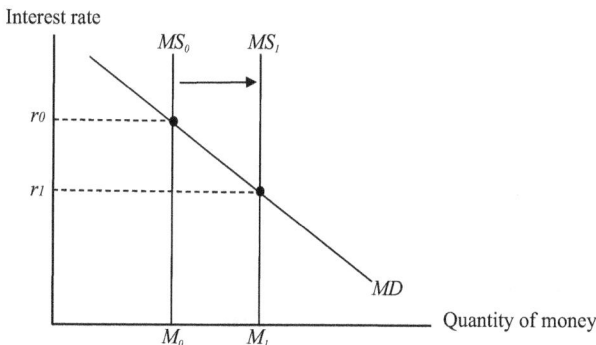

Figure 12.1 Increase in the money supply

lower interest rate encourages economic agents to hold the additional money the central bank creates, maintaining equilibrium in the market.

How does the change in the interest rate impact AD? The lower interest rate impacts the quantity of output demanded (Figure 12.2). A lower interest rate decreases the cost of borrowing. It also increases the reward for saving. Economic agents borrow more money, increasing their demand for goods and services. Households purchase new homes, increasing the demand for residential investment. Firms purchase more computers, equipment, and machinery, increasing the demand for business investment. The result of the monetary injection is that, at the given price level ($\bar{P}$), AD_1 shifts to AD_2, increasing the quantity of output demanded from Q_1 to Q_2.

In sum, when the central bank increases the money supply, the interest rate decreases. At $\bar{P}$, the lower cost of borrowing leads to an increase in the quantity of output demanded. The AD curve shifts to the right. In contrast, when the central bank decreases the money supply, the interest rate increases. At $\bar{P}$, the higher cost of borrowing leads to a decrease in the quantity of output demanded. The AD curve shifts to the left.

MONETARY POLICY AND ECONOMIC SHOCKS

The above discussion on monetary policy demonstrates the ways in which the central bank may achieve both short-run and long-run

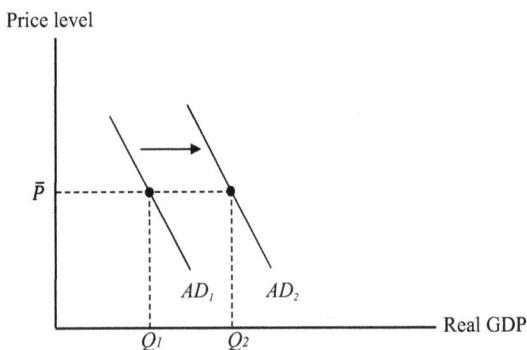

Figure 12.2 Increase in aggregate demand

goals. In the short run, the central bank prioritizes income and output. In the long run, the central bank prioritizes price-level stability.

In the latter context, price-level stability establishes an environment for economic growth. But in the short run, demand and supply shocks necessitate different approaches. The chosen approach depends on whether the focus is on the price level or income, and whether the shock stems from the aggregate demand or aggregate supply side of the economy.

With a demand shock, a decrease in AD results from a reduction in consumption, investment, government expenditure, or exports. During the Great Recession, households reduced spending in response to the crisis. In Figure 12.3, the decrease in AD_0 to AD_1 shifts the market from equilibrium point a to b, reducing output below the full employment level of production (Q_f) and increasing the unemployment rate. What is the central bank's response? An expansionary policy increases the money supply, decreases the interest rate, shifts AD_1 back to AD_0, and re-establishes the economy at Q_f.

With a supply shock, a decrease in $SRAS$ may result from higher inflationary expectations, an increase in the market power of firms, a higher price for economic resources, or a change in another factor. In Figure 12.4, when $SRAS_0$ shifts left to $SRAS_1$, the equilibrium moves from point a to b, and the economy falls below Q_f. But a new problem exists: inflation. The price level (P_1) is greater than $P^\star$.

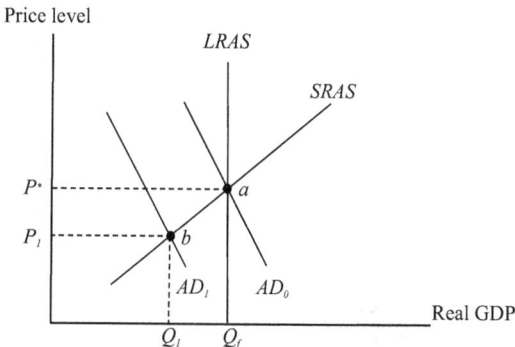

Figure 12.3 Central bank response to a demand shock

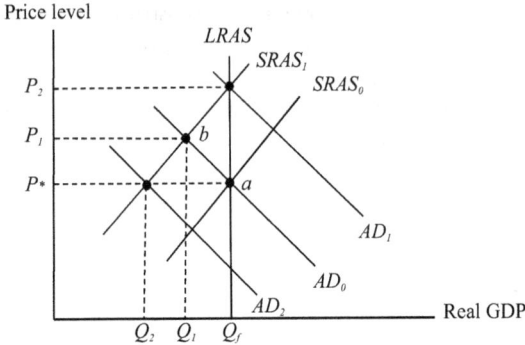

Figure 12.4 Central bank response to a supply shock

What is the policy response? The choice is difficult for the central bank. It must decide which problem to address: inflation or unemployment. Expansionary monetary policy shifts AD_0 rightward to AD_1, but adds to the inflationary pressure. Contractionary monetary policy shifts AD_0 leftward to AD_2, returning the price level to $P^{\star}$, but further decreasing the production of output. The latter outcome leads to a higher unemployment rate.

In the late 1970s, many countries faced this problem, because of the rise in global energy prices and a decrease in $SRAS$. The US central bank implemented contractionary monetary policy to fight inflation, raising the interest rate, but making the recession persist. It took a long time for the economy to recover. Given an economy characterized by stagflation—rising inflation and unemployment—central banks normally choose to fight inflation, hoping a stable price level will lead to economic growth.

THE ROLE OF INTEREST RATE TARGETS

How does the central bank impact the economy? The above discussion reveals that changes in the money supply serve as the central bank's main policy instrument. When the central bank buys bonds in the open market, the money supply increases and AD shifts to the right. When the central bank sells bonds in the open market, the money supply decreases and AD shifts to the left. But the central bank often views the interest rate, rather than the money supply, as a policy target.

Central banks establish the reserve requirements for commercial banks. This law establishes fractional reserve banking, when banks expand demand deposits through loans. Banks hold both required reserves and excess reserves. The reserves are held as vault cash or in accounts with the central bank. The banks use the accounts to meet the reserve requirement and clear banking transactions.

But if the accounts at the central bank are overdrawn at the end of the day, the central bank assesses a penalty. Given both this possibility and the volume of daily banking transactions, many commercial banks maintain excess reserves. At the end of the day, if a bank is overdrawn, it may borrow reserves from other banks.

In this context, the *federal funds rate* is the cost of borrowing. It is the interest rate that commercial banks charge each other for overnight loans that are used as reserves. A change in the federal funds rate reflects changes in the supply of and demand for excess reserves. An increase in the demand for excess reserves will increase the federal funds rate. A decrease in demand will have the opposite effect.

In the US, a committee of the Federal Reserve System—the central bank—establishes a target for the federal funds rate, which serves as a guide for the central bank's stance on monetary policy. Every six weeks, the Federal Open Market Committee (FOMC) evaluates the state of the economy and adjusts the target federal funds rate. For example, when the FOMC observes a strong economy with low unemployment and stable inflation, it maintains the federal funds rate. But a rising unemployment rate establishes a signal to decrease the rate, lowering the cost of borrowing between banks, increasing the availability of loanable funds, and stimulating economic activity. A rising inflation rate signals to the FOMC to increase the rate, raising the cost of borrowing between banks, decreasing the availability of loanable funds, and slowing the economy. A lower rate signals an easing of monetary policy. A higher rate signals a tightening of monetary policy.

To meet the target federal funds rate, the central bank adjusts its monetary policy. When it wants to lower the rate, it buys securities in the open market, increasing the *MS*. If it wants to raise the rate, it sells securities in the open market, decreasing the *MS*. Even though the central bank wants to maintain the federal funds rate within the target range, it does not always achieve the goal. Deviations result from bank behavior, market conditions, and unexpected events.

THE EUROZONE AND EUROPEAN CENTRAL BANK

In 1992, twelve European countries established the Eurozone, an area that would adopt a single currency, enhance trade, and set monetary conditions. The countries established criteria for members: low inflation, interest rates, budget deficits, and government debt. In 1999, when the euro was launched, eleven of the twelve countries met the criteria. In the third decade of this century, twenty countries use the euro.

The euro has become an important currency among global financial institutions. But by giving up their own currencies, the countries gave their monetary oversight to the European Central Bank, which is in Frankfurt, Germany.

During the Great Recession, several of the Eurozone countries experienced rising debt loads, requiring the selling of securities to prevent rising debt-to-GDP ratios. In response, the European Central Bank bought government debt, provided loans to banks, and managed the euro.

The challenge for the central bank is the economies of individual countries differ with respect to employment and inflationary conditions. But the countries do not have the ability to establish their own monetary policies. They must adopt the single policy of the European Central Bank. This is the reason that the countries must meet specific economic conditions.

By establishing one monetary policy in the Eurozone, the benefits of the system include the comparison of prices between countries, ease of trade, economic integration, efficient financial markets, influence in the global economy, and price-level stability. Because the European Central Bank implements monetary policy for the Eurozone, it reacts to ongoing economic challenges.

THE FEDERAL RESERVE SYSTEM (FED)

Established by the Federal Reserve Act of 1913, the Fed serves as an independent central bank of the US. It conducts monetary policy, establishes the money supply, and adjusts interest rates. Because of the Fed's preeminent position, it has enormous power to create money. Even though its policy decisions are independent of the executive branch of the federal government, its chair and governors are appointed by the president and approved by Congress. Presidents may disagree with the Fed's policy decisions. But the Fed argues for its independence.

The structure of the Fed includes: a Board of Governors, which is responsible for establishing and guiding monetary policy; twelve regional banks, which supervise financial institutions and provide banking services; and the FOMC, which conducts open market operations. In the banking system, the Fed is the lender of last resort, providing loans to banks in crisis, operating the discount window, and overseeing the monetary system.

The Fed's record in addressing economic crises is mixed. In response to the Great Recession, it lowered interest rates, provided liquidity, and established a policy of quantitative easing. In response to the coronavirus pandemic, it lowered interest rates, purchased assets, injected liquidity into the economy, and provided forward guidance. While the economic recovery from the Great Recession was slow, the recovery from the pandemic was more rapid, even though inflationary pressures emerged.

KEY TERMS

contractionary monetary policy
discount rate
expansionary monetary policy
federal funds rate
open market operations
yield

FURTHER READING

Bernanke, Ben. 2020. "The New Tools of Monetary Policy." *American Economic Review*, 110 (4): 943–983.

Brusa, Francesca, Savor, Pavel and Wilson, Mungo. 2020. "One Central Bank to Rule Them All." *Review of Finance*, 24 (2): 263–304.

Mosser, Patricia. 2020. "Central bank responses to COVID-19." *Business Economics*, 55 (4): 191–201.

PART VI

INTERNATIONAL ECONOMICS

INTERNATIONAL TRADE

BREXIT AND TRADE FLOWS

The exit of the United Kingdom (UK) from the European Union (EU), which occurred on January 31, 2020, resulted from a vote that took place in 2016. On June 23 of that year, the Leave vote established a mandate for the country to leave the EU's *trade agreement*, an outcome known as Brexit. A trade agreement includes countries that establish a method of economic integration, such as the reduction of trade barriers and the promotion of free trade.

When the UK left the EU, the UK experienced a higher level of sovereignty over its economic position. But the choice created several challenges with trade, immigration, and the business environment. With trade, higher trade barriers with the EU increased transaction costs and created uncertainty for future trading partners. With immigration, the end of the free movement of labor resources led to labor shortages in the UK. With the business environment, a different economic landscape impacted supply chains and productivity. The Brexit decision was the largest reversal of economic integration for a country in a trading bloc.

The decision highlights the importance of international trade, which is the study of the exchange of goods and services between countries. The chapter explores the reasons for trade, the policies that govern trade, and the economic implications of trade flows.

Since World War II, global trade flows have increased significantly, due to technological advancements and *trade liberalization* (the process of reducing or removing the barriers to trade). The

DOI: 10.4324/9781003678700-19

result is more competitive global markets, an increase in exports and imports, and a higher level of specialization.

But challenges include vulnerability to economic shocks, such as financial crises and pandemics, supply chain shortages, and *protectionism*, when countries implement domestic policies that discourage trade and promote domestic industries. Between 1985 and 2025, the global population increased from 4.87 billion to 8.2 billion. During the same time, the volume of global GDP quadrupled. The period is characterized by an increase in trade agreements, global trade flows, and economic integration.

Because international trade serves as an important component of macroeconomics, this chapter discusses trade flows, global supply chains, the motivation to trade, comparative advantage, terms of trade, protectionism, trade barriers, trade agreements, and the costs of international trade.

TRADE FLOWS

Economic agents around the world conduct business with each other because they expect to experience economic gains. At the country level, imports, which are goods and services purchased from foreign sellers, include many items, such as artwork, automobile parts, cars, cell phones, clothes, computers, electronics, food, and shoes. These items diversify a country's economy by providing consumers with a variety of products. But countries import services as well as goods. If an individual in the UK flies to the US on an American airline, the individual is importing a transportation service. In the UK, the top imports include electrical and electronic equipment, mechanical appliances, fossil fuels, precious metals, and vehicles. Imports are a function of consumer tastes and preferences, income, and purchasing power.

Exports, the goods and services sold to foreign buyers, vary according to economic conditions. Some countries have significant export-driven economies with higher exports-to-GDP ratios. Examples include the Netherlands, Mexico, Singapore, South Korea, and Switzerland. Export-driven economies attract foreign investment, create jobs, diversify markets, increase foreign exchange, and transfer knowledge. Today, most countries have open economies with exports and imports. Very few countries have closed economies without foreign trade. At the macro-economic level, a difference exists between the *balance of trade* and *level of trade*.

The balance of trade is the difference between the value of exports and imports. With a trade surplus, exports are greater than imports. In this case, a positive inward flow of revenue exists. When exports are less than imports, a trade deficit exists. The UK and the United States (US) normally experience annual trade deficits. But consumers are purchasing a greater variety of goods and services, leading to a downward pressure on prices.

The level of trade measures an economy's exports as a percentage of GDP. The variable is a function of an economy's location, productivity, and trade history. A country with a high level of trade, such as Belgium, Ireland, and Luxembourg, are integrated with other economies.

GLOBAL SUPPLY CHAINS

The last decades of the twentieth century and early decades of the twenty-first century experienced an expansion of *global supply chains* in international locations, including apparel, automobile, computer, and electronics markets. Global supply chains are networks that connect firms across national boundaries. They include the extraction of raw materials and procurement of economic resources, logistical options for suppliers, movement of economic resources to manufacturers, shipping from distributors, market conditions for retailers, and purchasing by consumers. The growth in global supply chains is a function of international trade flows and the process of *globalization*, the growing interdependence of the world's economies.

Because global supply chains transcend national boundaries, they pose challenges for business managers, who oversee new and existing product lines. The challenges include changing market conditions, material scarcity, transportation costs, new trade barriers, communication among partners, forecasting demand conditions, congestion, labor shortages, the incorporation of artificial intelligence, supplier relationships, and the difficulty of using multiple suppliers and distributors. Additional challenges include the design and location of production facilities, cost of economic resources, link between output markets and production locations, and the selection of suppliers for assembly.

International sources for manufacturing characterize the modern age. The reasons are labor costs, the bundling of suppliers, and reliability. But global supply chains impact the degree to which economies create a competitive advantage. In addition, global supply chains are a function of unique economic risks, including external shocks (financial crises, pandemics), currency volatility, economic and political instability, and changes in the rules and regulations for trade. The process of outsourcing manufacturing to foreign suppliers also characterizes the modern age. The suppliers are normally chosen on the basis of their ability to meet delivery, price, quality, quantity, and service needs. Even though supply chain management prioritizes cost reduction, the process enhances market flexibility, reliability, and responsiveness.

Ultimately, the integration of decisions across global supply chains influences the degree to which the process facilitates trade flows. The firms that evolve through artificial intelligence, innovative management techniques, and optimal logistical functions create profits from global supply chains.

MOTIVATION TO TRADE

The motivation to trade is important in the analysis of international economics. Many countries export some of the same products that they import. For example, the UK exports and imports vehicles in the process of two-way trade. The UK exports mini-models, hybrids, and luxury vehicles to the EU. In turn, the UK imports vehicles from Belgium, Germany, Spain, and other countries. The idea is that, in a globalized world, vehicles are manufactured and assembled across several countries. The process of two-way trade enhances both consumption and manufacturing, impacting aggregate demand and aggregate supply.

In addition to two-way trade, many economies could produce the products that they import. But the idea to trade with other countries arises from the same motivation for economic agents to specialize: economic gains. The reason that individuals do not become self-sufficient is that they increase their standard of living through specialization. Individuals focus on one form of employment, and then purchase a variety of goods and services. Countries specialize in production and trade for additional goods and services. Specialization increases an economy's output.

Chapter 1 discusses the link between specialization and trade. When labor specializes, both the productive capacity and level of expertise increases. A country has a comparative advantage when it produces output at a lower domestic opportunity cost than its trading partners. Taiwan, for example, has a comparative advantage in the production of computer chips. For Taiwan, the comparative advantage results from the clustering of businesses, global importance of the industry, government support, manufacturing expertise, private investment, and technological leadership. By producing and exporting computer chips, Taiwan maintains a comparative advantage. Specialization and trade shifts the production possibility curve (PPC) outward, increasing an economy's production and consumption possibilities (Figure 13.1).

COMPARATIVE ADVANTAGE

Although international trade may benefit all trading partners, questions arise concerning which products to trade and on what terms. In the previous example, the UK both imports and exports vehicles. But the decision to export specific forms of output is based on comparative advantage, the relative cost of producing output.

If a country produces specific goods or services at a lower domestic opportunity cost than a trading partner, it has comparative advantage.

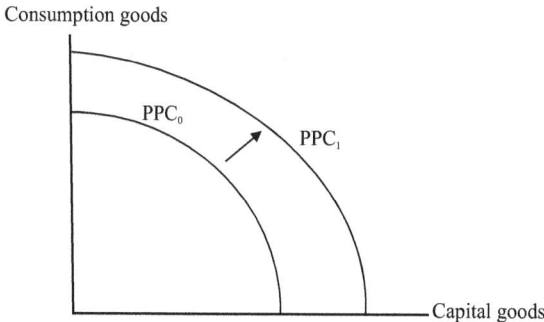

Figure 13.1 Trade increases an economy's production possibilities

The idea is that a country should specialize in the output that is relatively more efficient. This is the reason that Ecuador produces and exports bananas, Saudi Arabia produces and exports oil, and Taiwan produces and exports computer chips.

If each country produces according to comparative advantage and maximizes the gains from trade, global output grows. But each country must export the output with relatively low opportunity cost and import the output with relatively high opportunity cost. Two caveats exist.

First, countries should trade on the basis of comparative advantage, not absolute advantage. The latter exists when a country is able to produce more output with the same economic resources. The key for international trade is opportunity cost: what a country must give up in order to get more of a specific good. If one country can get more of good A by giving up less of good B than a trading partner, it has the motivation for trade. Some countries, such as China and the US, have absolute advantage in the production of many forms of output, because of their large economies. But the countries should not produce everything. They, too, should specialize, according to the relative cost of production.

Second, in specific industries, international trade leads to job losses and higher levels of income inequality. Industries that struggle to compete on a global scale may shed jobs, leading to hardships for communities and workers. If trade benefits some workers at the expense of others, a higher level of income inequality results from the disparity. All else equal, export industries may experience wage gains, relative to other industries. On balance, most economists agree that international trade benefits trading partners, but acknowledge that some communities, industries, and workers do not benefit from the process.

TERMS OF TRADE

While comparative advantage forms the basis for trade, the *terms of trade* refers to the rate at which goods are exchanged. A country will not trade unless the terms of trade are better than domestic opportunities. If the terms of trade offer higher economic gains, the country should trade with a partner. Specifically, the final terms of trade between countries exist between their opportunity costs. But markets and prices influence the process.

The decisions of producers and consumers determine trade flows. While comparative advantage forms the theoretical basis for trade, consumers consider prices. They buy additional goods and services with the highest level of marginal utility per dollar (or euro) spent. Producers focus on the prices they receive. Given their cost structures, producers maximize profit. On both sides of the market, the economic agents try to maximize the gains from trade.

An entrepreneur in France may notice that, while domestic wine is relatively cheap and furniture is relatively expensive, the opposite is true in the US. Exporting wine to the US and importing furniture to France takes advantage of the relative price differential. For the entrepreneur, it also creates the opportunity of profit. For the countries, the entrepreneurial decision leads to comparative advantage. The economic agent who makes the decision is not the secretary of trade in the federal government, but an enterprising individual. On both sides of the Atlantic, producers and consumers benefit. Where the terms of trade and the volume of trade finalize depends on three factors: entrepreneurial ability, market participants, and relative prices. The final terms of trade depend on the willingness of market participants to buy and sell output.

PROTECTIONISM

Even though an argument exists for international trade, it does not benefit everyone. Protectionism means that countries shield their domestic industries from foreign competition. Several reasons exist.

First, international trade opens foreign markets. But countries import goods and services from outside their borders. Domestic manufacturers may object. They may argue that it is important to maintain strong domestic industries. Firms in the import-competing industries may lobby the political system to raise awareness of their livelihoods. Even though consumers benefit from lower prices, the same individuals may not benefit if they struggle with employment. Unless the economy is creating jobs in other sectors, they may not be able to find work.

Second, although imports translate into fewer jobs and lower income in some domestic industries, export industries increase jobs and income. As a result, the firms and laborers in export industries gain from trade. International trade therefore alters the mix of output, redistributing income to export industries from import-competing industries.

Third, an argument against free trade stems from the process of *dumping*. Foreign suppliers dump their products on other countries when they sell them at prices below market equilibrium. The prices may even be lower than the cost of production. Why does dumping exist? Foreign suppliers dump products in domestic markets to gain market share. The process harms domestic industries who cannot compete.

Fourth, importing complicates the development of new industries. The *infant industry argument* states that countries should protect new industries from foreign competition. If the industries have time to develop, the argument goes, they will increase efficiency, decrease production costs, and implement technological advances. If import restrictions occur, the industry grows over time. The domestic firms then compete in global markets. Examples of infant industry protection include computers, solar panels, and vehicles. A problem exists when countries maintain infant industry protection over time, shielding the firms from competition.

In a macro context, the gains from trade exceed the losses. International trade leads to a higher level of output. Consumers benefit from a wider variety of products, at lower prices. Trade increases the efficiency of global trade. World output rises. Economies distribute a larger economic pie. But protectionism exists. The gains from trade do not accrue to all workers. How economies distribute the gains from trade serves as an important factor in the process.

TRADE BARRIERS

Trade policy includes the laws and regulations that govern trade flows. When countries restrict trade for protectionist sentiments or the protection of domestic industries, they implement trade policies. Each policy has a unique method of restricting imports.

An *export subsidy* encourages the export of goods or services through financial assistance to domestic firms or industries. The government implements the subsidy as either a fixed sum per unit of output or a proportion of the value of the product. The types of export subsidies include cash grants, direct payments, loans, and tax breaks. Even though the export subsidy lowers the price for foreign importers, domestic consumers pay a higher price. In the exporting country, the government pays the subsidy. But the policy increases the flow of exports to foreign countries.

An *import quota* restricts the quantity of imports. By requiring import licenses, the government restricts the flow of imports. With the policy, economic agents must hold an import license to import a particular good. The idea is that the license holder purchases imports from foreign countries and sells them at higher prices in domestic markets. In many countries, examples include import quotas on food, drinks, and other forms of output. Although the quota restricts specific imports, it increases the domestic prices. But the import quota does not generate revenue for the government. The revenue flows to the holder of the import license.

A *tariff* is a tax on imports, implemented to decrease imports, protect infant industries, and/or raise revenue for the government. The tariff is either a fixed sum per unit or a proportion of the value of the product. Firms that import products from other countries initially pay the tariff. When the product arrives at customs, the importer pays the tax to the customs agent. But the importer then passes the tax to consumers, absorbs some of the cost, or negotiates with the exporter to decrease the initial price. A tariff serves as a trade barrier, reducing the variety of goods and services available in domestic markets. It also applies to industries that import components and parts, leading to job losses. A tariff may establish a context for retaliation by foreign countries, or even trade wars. But a tariff may realign trade flows, stimulate investment in domestic industries, and create jobs in specific sectors.

A *voluntary export restraint* exists as a self-imposed limit for the amount of a product that is exported. A famous case is the self-imposed limit in the 1980s by Japan of vehicle exports to the US. Japan implemented the restraint to realign trade flows with an important trading partner. At the time, the Japanese automobile industry served as a threat because of its ability to produce cheaper and more fuel-efficient vehicles. The government of the US pressured Japan to implement the voluntary export restraint, rather than impose tariffs on Japanese imports. In general, the exporting country chooses to apply the voluntary export restraint when it fears a more severe trade restriction.

TRADE AGREEMENTS

Trade agreements between countries increase exports and imports by establishing trade guidelines. The guidelines determine the rules of trade and flow of economic resources. In 1994, Canada, Mexico, and the United States established the North American Free Trade Agreement (NAFTA). The purpose of the agreement was to eliminate most trade barriers between counties, increasing economic integration. But in 2020 the countries created the US-Mexico-Canada Agreement, which retained the main provisions of NAFTA, while updating digital trade, dispute resolution, intellectual property, labor standards, and other areas. The agreement strengthened ties between the countries. It did not, however, eliminate the possibility of new trade restrictions, such as the tariffs implemented by the United States in the mid-2020s.

To increase trade flows, a country implements trade agreements with other countries. The agreements increase the ability to compete on a global scale by providing access to new markets. The agreements increase the variety of goods and services in the marketplace, transparency, and volume of trade. Many trade agreements go beyond trade flows, addressing competition, environmental quality, intellectual property rights, and investment. Trade agreements establish different levels of economic integration between countries:

- Preferential trading area: member countries reduce or eliminate trade barriers with other members, but not with other countries
- Free trade agreement: broader in scope than a preferential trading area, member countries reduce or eliminate almost all trade barriers
- Customs union: member countries decrease administrative costs and eliminate trade barriers such as customs duties (tariffs on output that crosses country borders)
- Common market: as a trading bloc, member countries facilitate trade with other members, and allow the exchange of economic resources, such as labor and capital
- Economic union: member countries eliminate trade barriers with other members, allow the free flow of economic resources, and coordinate economic policies
- Monetary union: member countries add a common currency and monetary policy to the economic union

COSTS OF INTERNATIONAL TRADE

International trade serves as an important part of macroeconomies. It increases consumption opportunities, integrates economies, and enhances the ties between countries. But costs exists. Contract enforcement, information gathering, trade barriers, transaction costs, and transportation expenses characterize the process. Two other costs exist: income inequality and job displacement.

A country's income distribution is how total income is divided among its people. While no country has an equal income distribution, the variable is a function of several factors, including capital gains (income from financial investments), economic growth, education and skills, government policies, and labor market dynamics. A country with a low level of income inequality provides opportunities for all members of the population. With an unequal distribution of income, some members of the population benefit more than others from the existing economic and social order.

To address the problem, governments transfer funds from the private sector to the public sector through the process of taxation, and then redistribute money. *Redistribution* means altering the distribution of income from the market outcome to a different outcome. Governments adopt economic policies such as progressive taxation to redistribute income. In the process, societies empower governments to use the tax system to fund programs that benefit members of lower-income quintiles. Considering the costs that poverty and a widening income gap impose on economies, many governments close the gap between the rich and the poor.

How does international trade link with income inequality? The growth of world trade impacts the distribution of income. An example is the growing exports of manufactured goods from developing economies. Until the 1970s, international trade between advanced countries and developing countries consisted of an exchange of manufactured goods from the former for raw materials from the latter. But since the 1970s, many developing countries have been selling manufactured goods to advanced countries, such as the US and members of the EU. In the process, many developing countries moved from a traditional reliance on agricultural goods and mineral products to manufactured forms of output, such as electronics, machinery, and vehicles. Countries such as China and South Korea grew into manufacturing powers.

In advanced economies, a decrease in the demand for lower-skilled labor reduces wages, de-industrializes manufacturing sectors, leads to job displacement, and diminishes the economic prospects for many workers. The result, over time, is a rise in income inequality. Should advanced countries restrict trade with developing countries? While some believe the answer is yes, it is important to remember that international trade leads to both benefits and costs. The larger variety of consumer goods from international trade is weighed against the costs of international competition. International trade leads to the growth of certain sectors and decline of others. Trade policies guide the process, encourage specific markets, and facilitate trade flows.

KEY TERMS

balance of trade
dumping
export subsidy
globalization
global supply chains
import quota
infant industry argument
level of trade
protectionism
redistribution
tariff
terms of trade
trade agreement
trade liberalization
voluntary export restraint

FURTHER READING

Dorn, David and Zweimüller, Josef. 2021. "Migration and Labor Market Integration in Europe." *Journal of Economic Perspectives*, 35 (2): 49–76.

Dorn, Florian, Fuest, Clemens and Potrafke, Niklas. 2021. "Trade openness and income inequality: New empirical evidence." *Economic Inquiry*, 60 (1): 202–223.

Ganapati, Sharat and Wong, Woan. 2023. "How Far Goods Travel: Global Transport and Supply Chains from 1965–2020." *Journal of Economic Perspectives*, 37 (3): 3–30.

14

INTERNATIONAL FINANCE

EXCHANGE RATE FLUCTUATIONS

Trade flows help to determine an economy's position in the global economy. But currencies establish the value of the goods and services. In the context of international finance—the study of the monetary and macroeconomic interactions between economies—the challenge is that countries have different currencies. The members of the European Union that use the euro and trade with each other have an advantage: they have one currency. But when they trade with other countries, they must convert their home currencies into foreign currencies.

An *exchange rate* is the price of one currency in terms of another currency. The value of currencies, including the euro and dollar, fluctuates in the marketplace, according to supply and demand. For example, if the demand for euros rises, the euro experiences a process of *appreciation*, increasing in value. In contrast, if the demand for euros falls, the euro experiences a process of *depreciation*, decreasing in value.

What are the main drivers of variation in the exchange rate? First, in the interest rate channel, global investors increase their demand for euros if euro financial investments provide more interest than other assets. Second, in the risk premium channel, global investors demand euros when the currency appreciates during times of economic volatility. Third, in the convenience channel, global investors value euros for the safety and liquidity of euro-denominated assets. Together, the factors demonstrate the interconnectedness of both economies and currencies.

DOI: 10.4324/9781003678700-20

The point is that exchange rates are important for international trade. When a country's currency appreciates, its exports become more expensive. When a country's currency depreciates, its exports become less expensive.

When these changes occur, trade flows adjust. For example, during 2025, when the United States (US) implemented tariffs on many goods and services imported into the country, global investors questioned the safety and stability of the dollar. As a result, the dollar decreased in value, compared to the euro and other currencies. In particular, the higher value for the euro, compared to the dollar, attracted global investors. But as money flowed into euros and euro-denominated assets, exports from euro countries became more expensive.

As this example demonstrates, understanding how fluctuations in exchange rates impact trade flows serves as a fundamental part of international economics. To demonstrate the point, this chapter discusses the balance of payments, exchange rate determination, and government intervention in the foreign exchange market.

BALANCE OF PAYMENTS (BOP)

Open economies have BOP accounts. The first part of the BOP is the current account, including the payments for exports and imports, income flowing into and out of the country, and net transfers, such as foreign aid. The components of the current account are:

- Exports and imports: trade surplus or deficit
- Income: wages, rents, interest, and profits that domestic residents earn abroad minus the corresponding income foreign economic agents earn domestically
- Net transfers: foreign aid, funds sent to international organizations, stipends paid to foreign students studying domestically or domestic students studying abroad, and remittances of domestic residents working abroad
- Current account balance: surplus or deficit

The second part of the BOP is the capital account. It summarizes the flow of money into and out of domestic and foreign assets.

The change in foreign-owned assets includes investments in domestic plants and subsidiaries. Additional holdings of assets include foreign financial investments in domestic stocks, bonds, mutual funds, and holdings in domestic banks. The counterpart to this inflow of money occurs when domestic economic agents hold foreign financial assets in their portfolios.

Overall, when a country experiences a current account deficit, it has a capital account surplus. The reason is that the BOP must be balanced. A current account deficit means a country is importing more output and making more transfer payments than it is exporting output and receiving income from abroad. In addition, a capital account surplus means a net inflow of money. That is, foreign economic agents are purchasing more domestic assets than domestic residents are acquiring from abroad. In general, the money flowing into the country (capital account surplus) covers the spending on imports and other items (current account deficit).

EXCHANGE RATE DETERMINATION

In international economics, exchange rates are important because they impact the flow of exports and imports. The US imports products from the UK, including aircraft, cars, furniture, medical devices, pharmaceuticals, and many other items. Annually, the value of US imports from the UK is in the billions of US dollars.

EXPORTS FROM THE UK TO THE US

Suppose an individual in the US wants to import a piece of furniture from the UK.

While the furniture costs £1,000 in the UK, the importer will sell the item in the US. What is the dollar cost? To answer the question, the importer multiplies the pound price by the dollar/pound exchange rate. If the exchange rate is $0.75 per pound, the dollar price of the furniture is:(0.75 $£) × (£1,000) = $750But a new $£ exchange rate alters the dollar price. The market fluctuation is the reason that the exchange rate is linked to trade flows. If the pound depreciates, falling to 0.70 $£, the price of the furniture decreases in dollars:(0.70 $£) × (£1,000) = $700For the US importer, the item is cheaper, even when the price in £ remains the same. If the pound appreciates, rising to $0.80, the price of the furniture increases in dollars:$(0.80 \ \$£) \times (£1,000) = \$800$The implication is that a currency depreciation decreases the price of output for foreign buyers. But a currency appreciation increases the price of output for foreign buyers. In international economics, exchange rates are linked to trade flows.

EXPORTS FROM THE US TO THE UK

Exchange rate fluctuations alter the prices that economic agents in the UK pay for US products. Suppose an individual in the UK imports computers from the US, which are $750 each. When the exchange rate is $0.75 per pound, the price of a $750 computer in £ is:

$$(\$750) \ / \ (0.75 \ \$£) = £1,000$$

If the pound depreciates to $0.70, the dollar appreciates. The computer from the US is more expensive for the buyer in the UK:

$$(\$750) \ / \ (0.70 \ \$£) = £1,071$$

If the pound appreciates to $0.80 per pound, the dollar depreciates. The computer from the US is less expensive for the buyer in the UK:

$$(\$750) \ / \ (0.80 \ \$£) = £938$$

The point is that, when the home currency appreciates, exports become more expensive, but imports are less expensive. In contrast, when the home currency depreciates, exports become less expensive, but imports are more expensive. These principles guide trade flows.

EXCHANGE RATE EQUIVALENTS

The exchange rate may be written in terms of £ or dollars (Table 14.1). With the exchange rate equivalents, economists consider trade flows from the perspective of either the exporting or importing country.

Table 14.1 Exchange rate equivalents

Exchange rate in terms of one pound	*Exchange rate in terms of one dollar*
£1 = $0.80	$1 = £1.25
£1 = $0.75	$1 = £1.33
£1 = $0.70	$1 = £1.43

FOREIGN EXCHANGE MARKET

The foreign exchange market determines the exchange rates between currencies (Figure 14.1). The horizontal axis shows the quantity of dollars available for foreign exchange. The vertical axis shows the exchange rate in £ per dollar. The spot exchange rate that exists at a moment in time is the market equilibrium, the point at which the market balances. That is, the equilibrium is the rate in which the quantity of currency demanded equals the quantity of currency supplied. In the figure, the equilibrium exists at an exchange rate of £1.33 = $1. At a higher exchange rate, such as £1.43 = $1, the quantity supplied of dollars exceeds the quantity demanded. At a lower exchange rate, such as £1.25 = $1, the quantity demanded of dollars exceeds the quantity supplied.

The shapes of demand and supply stem from different economic factors. From the perspective of the UK, the demand for dollars is determined by economic agents in the UK either purchasing US goods and services or traveling to the US. The demand for dollars

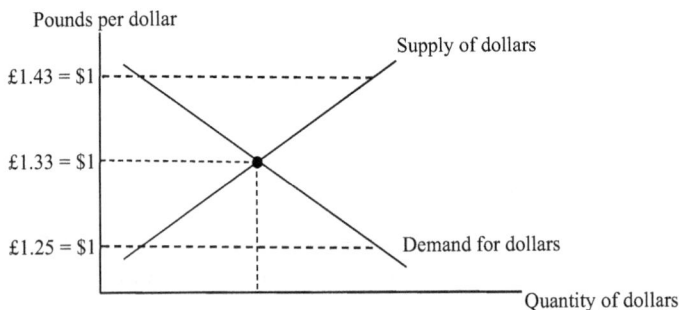

Figure 14.1 Foreign exchange market

as foreign exchange slopes downward. As the exchange rate falls and the dollar depreciates, US exports become more attractive in the UK. Economic agents desire more dollars. The upward-sloping supply of dollars is determined by the US central bank and the flow of UK exports to the US.

The demand side of the market includes central banks, commercial banks, firms, individuals, and nonbank financial institutions. They buy and sell foreign exchange. The demand for foreign exchange is similar to the demand for output. An economic agent purchases foreign exchange for economic transactions or speculation when the currency is forecasted to increase in value. In making the purchase of foreign exchange, the economic agent considers two factors: the potential change in value and the interest rate.

With the first factor, the potential change in currency value, economic agents estimate how many units of domestic currency they will eventually get back after the purchase of foreign exchange. For an economic agent in the US, suppose the pound appreciates, increasing in value from $0.70 per pound when the purchase occurs to $0.80 per pound when the selling occurs. If the agent buys low and sells high, a positive return will exist in dollars.

With the second factor, the interest rate, deposits in financial institutions pay interest. A deposit means an economic agent is lending currency to a financial institution. At an annual interest rate of 3 percent, a purchase of £1,000 would yield £1,030 after one year. When purchasing foreign exchange, economic agents consider the interest they receive.

When an exchange rate changes in value in the market, it is known as a *floating exchange rate*. In the global economy, this is the most common arrangement. Changes in the supply of or demand for foreign exchange determine whether a currency appreciates or depreciates in value.

CHANGE IN THE DEMAND FOR FOREIGN EXCHANGE

The demand for foreign exchange means the demand for another country's currency. The demand is a function of four determinants: the desire to purchase the foreign country's exports, domestic income, the foreign country's level of inflation, and the foreign country's interest rate. For example, if consumers in the UK purchase more exports from the US, the demand for dollars increases, shifting to the right. Moreover, if the growth in income in the UK exceeds the growth of income in other countries, the demand for imports into the UK increases faster than the demand for imports in other countries. Finally, if the US inflation rate falls or the US interest rate rises, the demand for dollars increases. In sum, the demand for foreign exchange is a function of:

- A change in domestic tastes and preferences for imports
- A change in domestic income
- A change in the foreign rate of inflation
- A change in the foreign interest rate

Suppose the latter scenario: the US interest rate rises, increasing the return on dollar-denominated assets. The demand for dollars in the UK increases from D_0 to D_1 (Figure 14.2). The dollar appreciates from £1.33 = \$1 to £1.43 = \$1. At the same time, the pound depreciates.

CHANGE IN THE SUPPLY OF FOREIGN EXCHANGE

From the perspective of the UK, the supply of US dollars comes from both the monetary policy of the US central bank and UK exports to the US. For example, when the Fed purchases government securities in the open market, the US money supply increases, shifting to the right. In addition, when the flow of UK exports

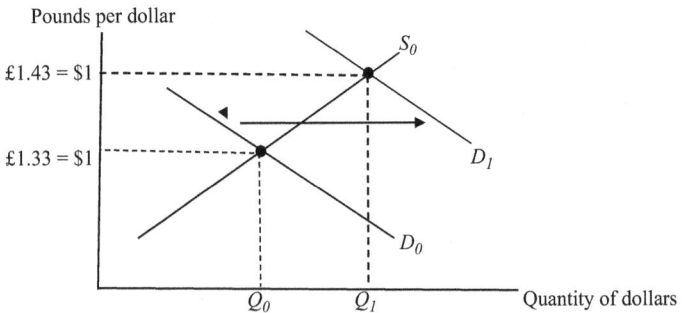

Figure 14.2 Increase in demand in the foreign exchange market

to the US rises, economic agents in the UK earn more dollars, and the supply of dollars increases. In sum, two factors alter the supply of foreign currency:

- A change in central bank policy of the foreign country
- A change in exports to the foreign country

Suppose exports increase from the UK to the US. In this situation, US consumers increase their tastes and preferences for products from the UK. Economic agents in the UK earn more dollars. In the foreign exchange market, the supply of dollars increases from S_0 to S_1 (Figure 14.3). The dollar depreciates from £1.33 = $1 to £1.25 = $1. At the same time, the pound appreciates.

EXCHANGE RATES AND THE CURRENT ACCOUNT

As this chapter explains, the current account includes payments for export and imports. The account also includes the changes in income that flow into and outside of the country. The exchange rate impacts both of these components.

Suppose the inflation rate rises in the UK, relative to the US. Because of the increase in production costs in the UK, goods and services are relatively more expensive. What is the result? Exports from the US to the UK rise, improving the US current account. Consumers in the US purchase more domestic output and fewer

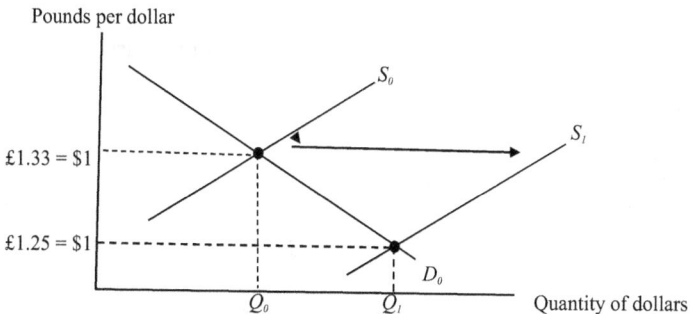

Figure 14.3 Increase in supply in the foreign exchange market

imports from the UK, further improving the US current account. But the opposite occurs for the UK: imports increase and exports decrease, hurting the current account in the UK.

Suppose an increase in income in the UK. Domestic consumers have more money to spend. At the existing exchange rate, imports increase, along with spending on other goods and services. The result of a higher level of imports is a worsening of the UK current account. In sum,

- An increase in inflation compared to other countries worsens the current account
- A decrease in inflation compared to other countries improves the current account
- An increase in income worsens the current account
- A decrease in income improves the current account

EXCHANGE RATES AND THE CAPITAL ACCOUNT

The capital account includes the flow of money into and out of domestic assets. Firms, governments, and individuals purchase stocks, bonds, companies, and real estate. The idea is that financial investors may purchase both foreign and domestic assets. The investment opportunities abroad include foreign direct investment, the purchase and sale of foreign financial assets, and the movement of money in foreign bank accounts. Because the transactions involve the flow of money, financial investors weigh the costs and benefits of their actions. The costs are measured in terms of risk. The benefits are measured in terms of return. In international finance, two factors are associated with risk and return: expected changes in the exchange rate and the interest rate.

Suppose a forecast for an appreciation of the pound. Financial investors in the US demand a higher return to offset the expected depreciation of the dollar. Unless the US interest rate rises, money will flow out of the US and into the UK. The process will continue until the interest rate in the UK falls enough to offset the expected appreciation of the pound.

If the exchange rate is constant between the UK and US, and financial investors substitute between the financial assets of the two countries, an increase in the interest rate in one country will attract the flow of money. For example, a rise in the interest rate in the UK will increase the flow of money from the US, where the interest rate has not changed. In the UK, financial investors will earn a higher rate of return.

EXCHANGE RATES, AGGREGATE SUPPLY (AS), AND AGGREGATE DEMAND (AD)

Changes in the exchange rate impact AS and AD. The pathway occurs through exports and imports. When the dollar appreciates, individuals in the UK purchase fewer dollars. What is the result? US exports decrease to the UK, reducing AD in the US. But some economic resources used in production are imported, including raw materials and parts. As a result, input costs fall in the US, increasing short-run aggregate supply ($SRAS$).

At point a in Figure 14.4, the US economy is initially operating at the full-employment level of output (Q_f) and price level ($P\star$). When the dollar appreciates, US exports decrease, AD_0 shifts leftward to AD_1, real GDP falls to Q_1, and the economy moves to point b. Because the economy imports some economic resources, $SRAS_0$ increases to $SRAS_1$, real GDP returns to Q_f, the price level decreases to P_2, and the economy moves to point c. The overall result is a decrease in the price level.

A currency appreciation leads to this outcome because imports become less expensive, while exports become more expensive. Consumers purchase more than before: the prices of domestic

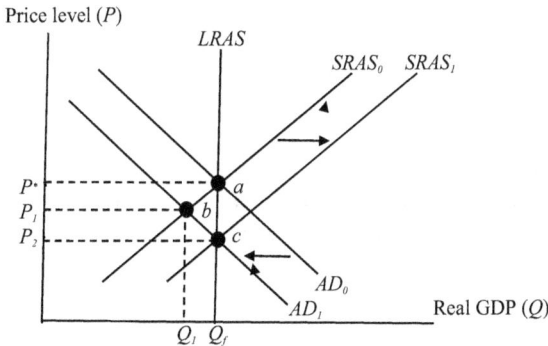

Figure 14.4 Exchange rates, AS, and AD

goods and services do not change. In economies where imports constitute an important part of household spending, a currency appreciation leads to a higher level of consumption.

GOVERNMENT INTERVENTION IN THE FOREIGN EXCHANGE MARKET

Given the impact of changes in the exchange rate on trade flows, governments often intervene in the foreign exchange market to stabilize the exchange rate. The objective is to increase the level of stability. The interventions, however, differ according to economic circumstances.

FLOATING EXCHANGE RATES

The global monetary system includes different types of exchange rate systems. But most countries have floating exchange rates. The currencies fluctuate according to the forces of supply and demand. The marketplace determines the change in currency values. At equilibrium, the quantity of foreign exchange demanded equals the quantity supplied. But floating exchange rates alter both relative prices and trade flows.

As this chapter explains, a currency depreciation increases the price of imports. The result is a contribution to cost-push inflation. Domestic firms that use imported resources in production or sell imported goods experience a decrease in sales. In contrast, an appreciation of the home currency increases the price of exports. Thus, with a change in currency value, some economic agents benefit while others experience a loss.

Government intervention takes the form of buying or selling foreign exchange. The central bank may sell foreign currency or buy domestic currency to increase its value. The central bank may buy foreign currency and sell domestic currency to decrease its value. In both cases, the change in the value of the domestic currency alters trade flows.

In a floating system, how does monetary policy impact the exchange rate? With constant fiscal policy, an increase in the money supply lowers interest rates, increases the outflow of money, and moves the BOP into a deficit. Both consumers and financial investors demand more foreign exchange. A home currency depreciation occurs. But with the depreciation, exports increase. As a result, the global economy reinforces the expansionary monetary policy.

Another option is to peg the home currency to a foreign currency, such as the US dollar or European euro. The reason is that a fixed exchange rate prevents fluctuations, thus stabilizing trade flows. As a variation, some countries do not maintain a fixed exchange rate with the dollar or euro, but intervene in the foreign exchange market to guide the exchange rate. China, for example, intervenes in the foreign exchange market to prop up the value of the US dollar. By holding dollars and not selling them in the foreign exchange market, China contributes to a stronger dollar. The result is that China keeps the prices of its exports to the US low.

Finally, some countries replace their home currency with a foreign currency. In a process known as *dollarization*, Ecuador, El Salvador, and Panama use the US dollar as their official currency. The benefit is the elimination of risk from a currency devaluation. The cost is the inability to use monetary policy in the foreign exchange market.

FIXED EXCHANGE RATES

Countries may eliminate volatility in the foreign exchange market by fixing the value of the domestic currency. In the past, the method was to set the value of the home currency in terms of a common standard. In the *gold standard*, the value of the currency was set according to a certain amount of gold.

In 1944, the major trading nations met in Bretton Woods, New Hampshire to establish a new monetary system. The system made the US dollar convertible into gold at $35 per ounce. As a result, the dollar was fixed at 0.0294 ounces of gold. The other currencies were fixed in value to the dollar. As a result, the currencies were convertible into each other. This meant that a person from the US who purchased British £ could sell them in the foreign exchange market for dollars, buy exports from the UK, or travel to the UK.

While the Bretton Woods system established the dollar as the world's main currency, the system did not eliminate market pressure. Countries struggled to maintain fixed exchange rates. The reason was that unpredictable market forces impacted currency values. Countries that wanted to stabilize the value of their currencies had to neutralize market forces.

In general, with fixed exchange rates, currency values do not adjust to changing market conditions. An increase in the demand for foreign exchange creates an excess demand. More units of the currency are demanded at the fixed exchange rate than are supplied. Domestic consumers want more units of the foreign currency. At the fixed exchange rate, the difference between the quantity demanded and quantity supplied is a market shortage of foreign currency. For the home country, the result is a BOP deficit. More units of domestic currency flow out of the country than into it. For the foreign country, the disequilibrium creates a BOP surplus: the outward flow of currency is less than the incoming flow.

What are the solutions? The home country must either allow the exchange rate to rise or alter market conditions so supply and demand intersect at a new exchange rate. If the exchange rate is fixed, the only option is the second choice. In particular, the central bank could supply the foreign currency to domestic consumers. The assumption is that the central bank accumulates foreign currency in earlier periods. By supplying the foreign currency, the central bank offsets the excess demand.

While the central bank uses the foreign exchange reserves to alter the exchange rate, it may not have an adequate supply of reserves. In response, gold could serve as a substitute for the reserves of foreign exchange. If the currency is tied in value to gold, the central bank could use gold to purchase foreign exchange. The problem is that the central bank must hold an adequate supply of gold. But the BOP deficit may exceed the quantity of gold held by the central bank.

With Bretton Woods, the advantages were the combination of the gold standard, fixed exchange rates, and the stability in the international monetary system. Member countries held international reserves in dollars or gold, maintaining the right to exchange dollars with the US central bank for gold.

Over time, however, inconsistencies persisted, including the inability of the US to hold a sufficient amount of gold. For member countries, the fixed exchange rates did not offer enough flexibility. As a result, the Bretton Woods system fell in 1973. Since that time, floating exchange rates have characterized the international monetary system.

KEY TERMS

appreciation
depreciation
dollarization
exchange rate
floating exchange rate
gold standard

FURTHER READING

Cipriani, Marco, Goldberg, Linda and La Spada, Gabriele. 2023. "Financial Sanctions, SWIFT, and the Architecture of the International Payment System." *Journal of Economic Perspectives*, 37 (1): 31–52.

Dellas, Harris and Tavlas, George. 2022. "Retrospectives: On the Evolution of the Rules versus Discretion Debate in Monetary Policy." *Journal of Economic Perspectives*, 36 (3): 245–260.

Obstfeld, Maurice and Taylor, Alan. 2017. "International Monetary Relations: Taking Finance Seriously." *Journal of Economic Perspectives*, 31 (3): 3–28.

GLOSSARY

absolute advantage the ability to produce more output using the same economic resources

adverse selection when an information imbalance leads one party to take advantage of another

aggregate demand total value of final goods and services purchased in the economy

aggregate supply total supply of goods and services available from producers

aggregate price level average of the prices of all goods and services in the economy

appreciation increase in currency value

asset transformation when riskier assets are transformed into safer assets

asymmetric information when one party in a transaction has more information than the other

automatic stabilizers government policies that automatically adjust spending and tax revenues to mitigate economic fluctuations

autonomous consumption spending that does not depend on income

average prices mean price over a period of time, calculated by dividing the total sum of all prices by the number of prices observed

average propensity to consume fraction of disposable income spent on consumption

average propensity to save fraction of disposable income saved

balance of trade difference between the value of exports and imports

DOI: 10.4324/9781003678700-21

base period a period of time serving as a point of reference

bitcoin cryptocurrency designed to act as money and a form of payment

blockchain decentralized, distributed digital ledger that serves as a record of transactions

bonds debt instruments where economic agents lend money to borrowers for set periods at a fixed interest rate

business cycle recurring pattern of economic expansion and contraction

capital factor of production that includes manufacturing resources such as buildings, equipment, and machinery that are used to produce other goods and services

capital depreciation decline in the value of capital assets over time

capital market where debt instruments with maturities longer than one year and equities are bought and sold

capitalism economic system in which economic agents own the means of production and use it for profit

catch-up effect theory that poorer countries will grow faster than richer countries, eventually closing the gap in per capita income

ceteris paribus all else equal

circular flow of economic activity model that illustrates the continuous movement of money, economic resources, and output between households and firms in the economy

closed economies economic systems that do not conduct trade with other countries

collective bargaining process when a union or other employee organization negotiates with an employer over working conditions and wages

comparative advantage when a country produces output at a lower domestic opportunity cost than a trading partner

constant opportunity cost when the sacrifice of one good for another remains constant

Consumer Price Index measures the change over time in the prices paid by urban consumers for a fixed basket of goods and services

contractionary fiscal policy when less government expenditure or higher taxation decreases economic activity

contractionary monetary policy when a decrease in the money supply reduces economic activity

core inflation measure of the price trends in the economy, excluding the prices of food and energy

cost-push inflation type of inflation that occurs when the overall cost of production rises

crowding out when increased government spending or borrowing reduces private sector spending and investment

cyclical deficit part of the government budget deficit that arises due to the state of the business cycle, specifically the contraction

cyclical unemployment job losses from an economic contraction

debt instruments financial instruments that serve as loans, obligating the issuers to repay specific amounts of principal plus interest

debt-to-GDP ratio metric that compares debt to economic output

deflation general decrease in the price level

demand for loanable funds total amount of money that economic agents want to borrow

demand-pull inflation type of inflation that occurs when aggregate demand outpaces the economy's ability to supply goods

depreciation decrease in currency value

digital currency money existing in electronic form

discount rate interest rate used to calculate the present value of future cash flows

discouraged worker someone who is available for work but has stopped seeking employment

disposable income amount of income left after paying taxes

dividends distributions of a portion of the earnings of companies to their shareholders

dollarization when a country adopts a foreign currency, such as the US dollar

double coincidence of wants barter system where two parties must possess the goods or services that the other wants to facilitate trade

dumping when a firm or country exports a product to another country at a price lower than its domestic price or the cost of production

economic growth increase in the production of output

efficiency wages payments above the market-clearing wage

efficient when economic resources are allocated and used in a way that maximizes net benefits and minimizes waste

employment-to-population ratio percentage of the working age population that is employed

entrepreneurship economic force that drives innovation and growth

equities shares of ownership in a company, granting a claim on the company's assets and earnings

excess reserves difference between reserves and required reserves

exchange rate price of one currency in terms of another currency

expansionary fiscal policy when more government expenditure or less taxation increases economic activity

expansionary monetary policy when an increase in the money supply increases economic activity

export price effect when the price level falls and exports rise

export subsidy government policy that provides financial support to domestic producers to encourage them to export goods and services

factor markets input markets where factors of production are bought and sold

federal funds rate interest rate for overnight lending between banks

fiat money type of currency that has value because the government declares it legal tender

financial intermediaries institutions that facilitate the flow of money from savers to investors

financial markets mechanisms that channel funds from savers to borrowers

financial system group of institutions and markets that channels money from savers to investors

fiscal policy use of government spending and taxation to influence the economy

Fisher effect nominal interest rates adjust to reflect the expected rate of inflation

floating exchange rate when the exchange rate is determined by the forces of supply and demand

fractional reserve banking system where banks hold a portion of customer deposits in reserve

frictional unemployment type of temporary unemployment of workers between jobs or entering the job market for the first time

globalization growing global integration of companies, countries, and individuals

global supply chains networks that connect firms across national boundaries

gold standard monetary system where the home currency is fixed in value to gold

government outlays total expenditure by a government to meet its obligations

government purchases value of goods and services bought by government at all levels

Gross Domestic Product final value of goods and services produced in the economy in a year

gross private domestic investment total value of investment expenditures by the private sector

hyperinflation rapid increase in the price level

import quota restriction on the quantity of imports

increasing opportunity cost as more economic resources are dedicated to producing one form of output, the amount of the other form of output given up increases with additional units

infant industry argument countries should protect new industries from foreign competition

inflation increase in the price level

inflationary GDP gap when real GDP is higher than potential GDP

inflation rate ongoing rate at which the price level is rising

infrastructure physical and organizational systems that underpin the economy

injections additional spending into the circular flow of economic activity

intangible capital non-physical assets with value

interest rate effect how changes in the interest rate alter investment and spending

intermediate goods products or components used in the production of output

intertemporal substitution decision to shift consumption between different points in time

invisible hand of the market self-regulating nature of the free market economy

labor factor of production that includes the human physical and mental effort, time, and skill exerted in the production of output

labor force individuals who are employed or actively seeking work

labor force participation rate percentage of the working-age population either employed or seeking work

labor market factor market that brings together the demand for and supply of labor

labor productivity measure of the real output produced per labor hour

labor unions organizations of workers that use collective bargaining to negotiate benefits, wages, and working conditions

laissez-faire minimal government intervention in the economy

land factor of production that includes natural resources and geographic locations

leakages diversions of income from the circular flow of economic activity

level of trade exports as a percentage of GDP

liquidity ease with which economic agents convert assets into cash without a decrease in value

macroeconomics study of the economy as a whole

marginal propensity to consume change in consumption divided by the change in income

marginal propensity to save change in savings divided by the change in income

market mechanism that brings together buyers and sellers for the purpose of exchange

market mechanism process where the forces of supply and demand determine the prices and quantities of goods and services

medium of exchange something that is accepted as payment for goods and services

menu costs business expense that occurs when the prices of goods and services change

money market mechanism where short-term debt instruments of less than one year are bought and sold

money multiplier amount of money that the banking system generates with each dollar of reserves

moral hazard when one party in a transaction takes on more risk because they know the other party will bear the consequences

multiplier effect how an initial change in spending leads to a larger overall change in the economy

national income total final value of output produced in the economy in a year

national income accounts set of statistics that track economic activity

natural level of output maximum level of real GDP an economy can produce without generating inflationary pressures

natural rate of unemployment when unemployment is frictional and structural, but cyclical is equal to zero

net domestic product value of final goods and services in the economy minus capital depreciation

net exports value of exports minus imports

neutrality of money when changes in the money supply only impact nominal variables **nominal GDP** total value of final goods and services over a specific period of time in current prices

normative economics analysis that considers what ought to be

open economies economic systems that conduct trade with other countries

open market operations form of monetary policy of the central bank to buy and sell securities in order to alter the money supply

opportunity cost value of the best foregone alternative

personal consumption expenditure total value of output purchased by households in a period of time

Personal Consumption Expenditures Index measure of the spending by households on all goods and services, including the expenditures made on their behalf by firms

positive economics analysis that considers what is

price index measure that summarizes changes in the price level

primary market mechanism in which securities such as stocks and bonds are created and sold for the first time by the issuer

private savings portion of disposable income that is not spent on consumption or taxes

Producer Price Index measures the average change over time in the selling prices received by producers for their output

product markets mechanisms where final goods and services are exchanged

production function maximum amount of output from different combinations of economic resources and technology

production possibility curve model that demonstrates the maximum amount of output that an economy may produce, given the economic resources and production technology

production process method in which firms turn economic resources into output

production technology tools and techniques that produce goods and services

productivity measure of an economy's ability to produce output

protectionism government policies that restrict international trade

public savings government savings, calculated as total tax revenue minus total expenditures on goods, services, and transfer payments

quality of life concept that captures the well-being of a population

real GDP total value of final goods and services over a specific period of time in constant prices

real GDP per capita measure of total output, adjusted for inflation, divided by total population

real interest rate nominal interest rate minus the rate of inflation

recessionary GDP gap difference between actual GDP and potential GDP when the economy is operating below its potential

recessions significant downturns in the production of output

redistribution reallocation of income, wealth, or economic resources from one group to another

relative prices value of one good or service expressed in terms of another good or service

required reserves minimum percentage of bank deposits that must be held as reserves

Ricardian equivalence when consumers acting rationally save tax cuts they receive, anticipating future tax increases required to pay for government borrowing

risk potential that negative outcome will occur

Say's Law supply creates its own demand

secondary market where securities and other assets are traded that have already been issued by firms or governments

securities tradable financial assets

shoe-leather costs time and effort that is expended to manage and minimize the impact of inflation on the purchasing power of money

specialization practice of concentrating resources and efforts to produce a limited range of goods and services

stagflation economic condition characterized by stagnant economic growth and rising inflation

standard of living measure of well-being that is linked to a country's economic indicators

stock of capital collection of productive assets such as machinery and equipment that is used to produce goods and services

stocks claims of ownership of a company

storage medium resource or good that is held over time and retrieved for future use

store of value when a form of money maintains its value over time

structural deficit ongoing imbalance in the government budget where expenses exceed revenues

structural unemployment long-term condition from a mismatch between the skills of unemployed workers and the skills required for employment

supply of loanable funds total amount of money from savers that is available for lending and borrowing at different interest rates

tariff tax on imports

terms of trade rate at which goods are exchanged

time lag delay between a cause such as a policy action and its effect

total factor productivity measures how efficiently an economy uses its economic resources to produce output

trade agreement arrangement between two or more countries that establishes a method of economic integration, such as the reduction of trade barriers and the promotion of free trade

trade balance difference between the value of exports and imports over a specific period

trade deficit when imports exceed exports

trade liberalization reduction or removal of barriers to international trade

trade surplus when exports exceed imports

transfer payments movement of money or resources from government to individuals in which no goods, services, or efforts are required in return

underemployment when individuals are employed less than their full potential

unemployment rate percentage of the labor force that is jobless but actively seeking work

unit of account standard, monetary unit of measurement for prices and debts

unit-of-account costs expenses and inefficiencies that arise when currency is unreliable

velocity of money annual amount the average dollar changes hands

voluntary export restraint self-imposed limit for the amount of a product that is exported

wealth effect relationship between wealth and spending, where higher asset values make households feel wealthier, leading to higher spending

yield income from a financial investment, expressed as a percentage of cost or value

INDEX

For Product Safety Concerns and Information please contact our EU
representative GPSR@taylorandfrancis.com
Taylor & Francis Verlag GmbH, Kaufingerstraße 24, 80331 München, Germany